THE
MANAGEMENT
SCIENTIST

VERSION 5.0

FOR WINDOWS® 95, WINDOWS® 98, AND WINDOWS® NT

David R. Anderson
University of Cincinnati

Dennis J. Sweeney
University of Cincinnati

Thomas A. Williams
Rochester Institute of Technology

 South-Western College Publishing
an International Thomson Publishing company I(T)P®

Cincinnati · Albany · Boston · Detroit · Johannesburg · London · Madrid · Melbourne · Mexico City
New York · Pacific Grove · San Francisco · Scottsdale · Singapore · Tokyo · Toronto

Acquisitions Editor: Charles E. McCormick, Jr.
Developmental Editor: Alice C. Denny
Marketing Manager: Joseph A. Sabatino
Production Editor: Deanna R. Quinn
Manufacturing Coordinator: Dana Began Schwartz

Cover Design: Michael H. Stratton
Cover Photo: Mark Tomalty/Masterfile
Production House and Compositor: Cover to Cover
  Publishing, Inc.
Printer: West Group

International Thomson Publishing Europe
Berkshire House
168-173 High Holborn
London, WC1V7AA, United Kingdom

Nelson ITP, Australia
102 Dodds Street
South Melbourne
Victoria 3205 Australia

Nelson Canada
1120 Birchmount Road
Scarborough, Ontario
Canada M1K 5G4

International Thomson Publishing Southern Africa
Building 18, Constantia Square
138 Sixteenth Road, P.O. Box 2459
Halfway House, 1685 South Africa

International Thomson Editores
Seneca, 53
Colonia Polanco
11560 México D.F. México

International Thomson Publishing Asia
60 Alberta Street #15-01
Albert Complex
Singapore 189969

International Thomson Publishing Japan
Hirakawa-cho Kyowa Building, 3F
2-2-1 Hirakawa-cho, Chiyoda-ku
Tokyo 102, Japan

Library of Congress Cataloging-in-Publication Data
Anderson, David R., 19-- -
   The management scientist [computer file] / David R. Anderson,
Dennis J. Sweeney, Thomas A. Williams. -- Version 5.0 for Windows
95, Windows 98, and Windows NT.
   1 computer laser optical disc ; 4 3/4 in. + 1 user's manual.
   Also known as: Management scientist 5.0.
   System requirements: PC; 12MB RAM; Windows 95, Windows 98, or
Windows NT; VGA graphics; CD-ROM drive.
   Title from title screen.
   Ed. statement from user's manual t.p.
   Audience: College students.
   SUMMARY: Twelve menu-driven programs designed to solve a wide
variety of quantitative models for managerial decision-making for
students enrolled in quantitative methods and/or management science
courses. Modules include linear programming, transportation,
assignment, integer linear programming, shortest route, minimal
spanning tree, PERT/CPM, inventory, waiting lines, decision
analysis, forecasting, and Markov processes.
   ISBN 0324-00890-2 (package)
   ISBN 0-324-00892-9 (disc)
   ISBN 0-324-00889-9 (user's manual)
   1. Industrial management--Decision making--Mathematical models--
Software. 2. Industrial management--Linear programming--Software.
3. Statistical decision Software. I. Sweeney, Dennis J. II.
Williams, Thomas A., 19-- - III. Title. IV. Title: Management
scientist 5.0.
HD30.23 <1999 00609> <MRC>
658.4--dc13
                              99-20782

This book is printed on acid-free paper.

BRIEF CONTENTS

CONTENTS

PREFACE

This user's manual accompanies version 5.0 of *The Management Scientist*, a personal computer software package developed by David R. Anderson, Dennis J. Sweeney, and Thomas A. Williams. The software, developed to assist students enrolled in quantitative methods and management science courses, can be used to solve a wide variety of textbook problems as well as small-scale problems encountered in practice. Use of *The Management Scientist* demonstrates the valuable role of the computer in applying quantitative methods to decision problems.

The new version 5.0, available for Windows 95, Windows 98, and Windows NT environments, has a significantly improved user interface as well as more robust solution algorithms.

We take this opportunity to acknowledge the major contribution made by Amy Anneken in the development of Versions 4.0 and 5.0. Also, we are indebted to Daniel Joseph and Bradley Beck who assisted with previous versions of the software. At this time we do not know of errors but, of course, take responsibility for any that remain.

If you have any comments and suggestions regarding *The Management Scientist* software, we welcome your input. Please send comments and suggestions to

Dr. David R. Anderson
College of Business Administration
University of Cincinnati
Cincinnati, Ohio 45221-0130

David R. Anderson
Dennis J. Sweeney
Thomas A. Williams

January 1999

CHAPTER 1

INTRODUCTION

Welcome to version 5.0 of *The Management Scientist*. You are ready to install and begin using a PC software package designed to solve the following quantitative models for managerial decision making:

Linear programming
Transportation
Assignment
Integer linear programming
Shortest route
Minimal spanning tree
PERT/CPM
Inventory
Waiting lines
Decision analysis
Forecasting
Markov processes

You do not have to be an expert in quantitative analysis to use this software package. If you have a general understanding of the above types of problems, you simply select the program module that is appropriate for the problem you wish to solve. The corresponding chapter in this manual will guide you through an example problem and familiarize you with the data input, special features, and output information provided by the module. After following the step-by-step procedure for the example problem, you should be able to input, solve, and interpret the results for other problems that use that module.

1.1   USING THIS MANUAL

Most of us, after obtaining a new software package, would like to begin solving problems immediately; we do not want to read the complete manual just to get ready to use the software. The manual for *The Management Scientist* was prepared with this thought in mind. We recommend taking the following steps to minimize the start-up effort and thus be able to begin using the software as soon as possible.

1. Follow the directions in Section 1.2 to install *The Management Scientist* on a personal computer using Windows 95, Windows 98, or Windows NT.

2. Continue to read, or at least skim, the rest of Chapter 1 to obtain an overview of the entire software package and most of its features.

3. Select any one of the 12 modules of *The Management Scientist* to try. The chapters of the manual are independent of each other, so you should have no difficulty going directly to Chapter 9 if, for example, you want to use the inventory module first or going directly to Chapter 4 if you would like to try the assignment module. The discussion describing the module introduces you to the type of problems that can be solved and then shows you how to create and solve an example problem.

1.2   INSTALLATION

Version 5.0 of *The Management Scientist* will run on personal computers running Windows 95, Windows 98, or Windows NT. Installing the software on your computer is easy. Install *The Management Scientist* as follows:

1. Place the disk in the CD-ROM drive.

2. In Windows from the Start taskbar, choose **Run**.

3. On the Command line, type **D:\Setup**. If your CD-ROM drive is not D:, substitute the appropriate letter.

4. Click the **OK** button or press the **Enter** key.

5. Follow the prompts of the installation.

Running *The Management Scientist*

Once *The Management Scientist* has been installed it is ready to be used. To run MS 5.0 after it has been installed, go to **Programs** from the **Start** button. Go to The Management Scientist group and click on The Management Scientist, or its logo. The opening screen will then appear. Just click **Continue** to begin working with one of the 12 modules.

1.3   OVERVIEW OF THE SOFTWARE PACKAGE

The Management Scientist software package consists of 12 computer programs, called modules, that use quantitative methods to develop decision-making information. A brief description of each of the modules including problem-size information is provided below. More detailed information about each of the modules is presented in the remaining chapters.

Modules Available in *The Management Scientist*

Linear Programming. This program will maximize or minimize the value of a linear objective function subject to a set of linear constraints. The program can handle up to 100 variables and up to 50 constraints. Sensitivity analysis information is provided.

Transportation. This program will find the minimum cost or maximum profit schedule for the transportation of units from several supply origins to several demand destinations. Transportation problems with up to 30 origins and up to 30 destinations are permitted.

Assignment. This program will minimize the cost or maximize the revenue associated with assigning a set of agents to a set of tasks. Assignment problems with up to 30 agents and up to 30 tasks are permitted.

Integer Linear Programming. This program will solve all integer and mixed integer programming problems with up to 100 variables and 50 constraints. Both general integer and 0–1 variable problems can be solved. Data input and editing features are the same as for the linear programming module. Large numbers of integer variables significantly increase solution time.

Shortest Route. This program will find the shortest route between any two nodes of a network. Any node may be selected as the starting node and any other node may be selected as the ending node. The program will handle networks with a maximum of 20 nodes and a maximum of 40 arcs.

Minimal Spanning Tree. This program will find the minimal spanning tree for a network that has a maximum of 20 nodes and a maximum of 40 arcs.

PERT/CPM. This program will develop activity schedules for projects with up to 25 activities. Both the cases of certain activity times (single activity time estimates) and uncertain activity times (three activity time estimates) are allowed. The activity schedule, the critical activities, and the expected project completion time are computed.

Inventory. This program provides six inventory models that can be used to determine the optimal order quantity, the optimal reorder point, and related operating policies for a variety of inventory situations. Both the cases of deterministic demand and probabilistic demand are permitted.

Waiting Lines. This program will provide a summary of the operating characteristics of a variety of waiting line systems involving single and multiple channels. Operating characteristics such as average waiting time, average number of units in the system, probability of waiting, and so on are provided. An economic analysis of the waiting line may be conducted.

Decision Analysis. This program will provide the best decision alternative recommendation for problems having up to 10 decision alternatives, up to 10 states of nature and known or unknown state of nature probabilities. Up to 10 indicators may be considered in order to develop a decision strategy based on sample information. The expected values of perfect information and sample information are provided.

Forecasting. This program will compute forecasts for a time series by using either moving averages, exponential smoothing, trend projection, or trend and seasonal components. The mean square error measure of forecasting accuracy and forecasts for future time periods are provided. Time series with up to 100 data values or observations are permitted.

Markov Processes. This program will analyze Markov processes with up to 10 states. Both Markov processes involving steady state behavior and absorbing states can be analyzed.

1.4   USING *THE MANAGEMENT SCIENTIST*

This section describes the features of *The Management Scientist* that are found in all 12 modules. An overview of this section is recommended before you attempt to solve a problem using any of the modules.

Selecting a Module

After starting *The Management Scientist*, you will encounter the Select a Module menu shown in Figure 1.1. The choices provide access to the 12 modules. Click the desired module title and a brief description of the module will appear on the screen. To use the selected module simply click OK or, alternatively, double click the module title.

Creating a New Problem

Whenever you want to begin working on a new problem, choose the appropriate module and select the **File** pull-down menu shown in Figure 1.2. Then, selecting the option **New** will begin the problem description and data input process and allow you to create the new problem.

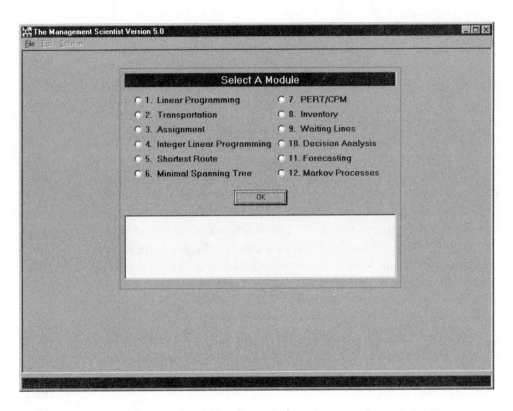

Figure 1.1   The Select a Module Menu

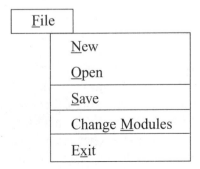

Figure 1.2   The File Pull-Down Menu

Saving a Problem

You may save a problem by selecting the **File** pull-down menu shown in Figure 1.2 and then selecting the **Save** option. This will enable you to name the problem and save it for later use. The Inventory and Waiting Line modules have a Save button directly on the data input dialog box. The Save button will enable you to save the problem without accessing the **File** pull-down menu.

After you specify the name of the problem, *The Management Scientist* automatically adds a three-letter extension. The extension is used to identify the module used to create the problem. For example, suppose you have a linear programming problem that you want to save using the name LPExample. *The Management Scientist* will add the extension LPM so that your problem will be saved as a file LPExample.LPM. Only files with the LPM extension can be saved and retrieved with the Linear Programming module. Other modules have their own three-letter extensions. While you can see the extensions on your directory of saved problems, you do *not* have to input the extensions because they are handled automatically by *The Management Scientist.*

Many users who elect to save problems find it a good file management practice to create a separate directory for saved problems. If you wish to do this, you will need to create your own problem directory. Then, whenever you select the Save option, you will be able to designate your problems directory as the place where you want to save the new problem. If you name the problems directory **Problems** and if it is a subdirectory of the directory containing *The Management Scientist*, *The Management Scientist* will automatically go to the Problems directory whenever you request Save.

Opening a Saved Problem

Suppose that you have previously saved a problem and that you now want to open the problem file so that the problem can be modified and/or solved again. Select the **File** pull-down menu shown in Figure 1.2 and then select the **Open** option. You will obtain a list of saved problems for the active module. Select the problem you want to open and it will appear on your screen ready for modification and/or solution.

Editing a Problem

Once you have created a new problem or opened a saved problem, you may make modifications, changes, or corrections right on the screen. If you have solved a problem and the solution is on the screen, you may go back and edit the problem by selecting the **Edit** pull-down menu shown in Figure 1.3. Selecting the **Display/Edit the Problem** option will display the problem's data input screen. You can use this screen to make changes to the problem. This editing process can be repeated any number of times, allowing you to learn how the solution changes as various aspects of the problem are modified.

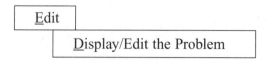

Figure 1.3   The Edit Pull-Down Menu

For most of the modules, the **Edit** pull-down menu only has the **Display/Edit the Problem** option. However, some of the modules have an additional editing option. For example, the Linear Programming and Integer Linear Programming modules have options on the **Edit** pull-down menu that allow you to change the number of variables and/or the number of constraints for the problem. The Transportation and Assignment modules also have **Edit** options that enable you to change the size of the problem.

Solving a Problem

When you have created a new problem, opened a saved problem, or edited a current problem, you will most likely want to solve it. Select the **Solution** pull-down menu shown in Figure 1.4. Then selecting **Solve** will solve the problem and display the solution on the screen. The Inventory and Waiting Line modules have a Solve button on the data input dialog box. In these modules, the Solve button will enable you to display the solution without accessing the **Solution** pull-down menu.

Printing a Solution

Once the solution appears on the screen, you may want to send it to a printer or to a text file. This is accomplished by selecting the **Solution** pull-down menu and then selecting the **Print Solution** option as shown in Figure 1.5. The **To Printer** or **To Text File** options indicate where the solution will be directed. A text file can be later accessed by a word processor so that the solution output can be edited and displayed as part of a solution report.

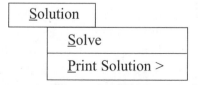

Figure 1.4   The Solution Pull-Down Menu

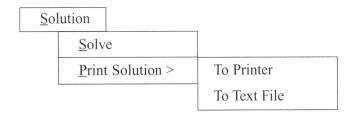

Figure 1.5   The Print Solution Pull-Down Menu

Changing Modules

After working with one module, you may want to change to a different module and solve another type of problem. Selecting the **File** pull-down menu and then selecting the **Change Modules** option will return you to the Select a Module screen shown in Figure 1.1. At this point, you may choose another module.

Exiting *The Management Scientist*

When you have completed a session with *The Management Scientist*, select the **File** pull-down menu and then select the **Exit** option.

1.5   OTHER CONSIDERATIONS

We have covered most of the general features of *The Management Scientist*. The following chapters contain more detailed information about particular modules. Each module chapter provides one or more example problems with a demonstration and discussion of data input, editing, special features, and output. The following additional comments and suggestions may be helpful as you use *The Management Scientist*.

Moving Around the Screen

In using *The Management Scientist* you will need to move around the screen in order to select menus and interact with data input dialog boxes. The mouse, the Tab key, and the arrow keys are the primary ways to navigate *The Management Scientist* package. Using the mouse provides the greatest degree of flexibility. Moving the mouse and clicking lets you move to any menu or cell on the screen. During sessions with data input and interactions with dialog boxes, the Tab key is very helpful. The Tab sequence is designed to move you through the most logical sequence of problem description and data input. After each piece of information is entered, the Tab key will signal the computer to accept the cell's input and move the cursor automatically to the next logical step of the input process. If the Tab key results in a move that is not where the user wants to go, the mouse can be used to reposition the cursor. The arrow keys may be used to navigate data input worksheets.

The mouse can be used to open the File, Edit, and Solution pull-down menus and to select options from the menus. In addition to the mouse, keystrokes can be used. The underlined letter in the menu or option title indicates the keystroke to use. Specifically, Alt-F will open the File pull-down menu, Alt-E will open the Edit pull-down menu, and Alt-S will open the Solution pull-down menu. Once a pull-down menu is opened, the Alt key is no longer required and the underlined letter for the desired option can be used. For example, in the **File** pull-down menu, N will activate New, O will activate Open, S will activate Save, M will activate Change Modules, and X will activate Exit.

Some Advice for Data Input

1. Do not enter commas (,) with your input data. For example, to enter the numerical value of 104,000, simply type the six digits 104000.

2. Do not enter the dollar sign ($) for profit or cost data. For example, a cost of $20.00 should be entered as 20.

3. Do not enter the percent sign (%) if percentage input is requested. For a percentage of 25%, simply enter 25. Do not enter 25% or .25.

4. Occasionally a quantitative model will be formulated with fractional values such as 1/4, 2/3, 5/6, and so on. The data input for the computer must be in decimal form. The fraction of 1/4 can be entered as .25. However, the fractions 2/3 and 5/6 have repeating decimal forms. In cases such as these we recommend the convention of rounding to 5 places. Thus, the corresponding decimal values of .66667 and .83333 should be entered.

5. Finally, we recommend that in general you attempt to scale extremely large or extremely small input data so that numbers of roughly the same magnitude may be input and operated on by the computer. For example, a cost of $2,500,000 may be scaled to 2.5 with the understanding that the data used in the problem reflect millions of dollars.

Special Error Messages

All modules check input data for validity before proceeding. If data input is not acceptable to the module, the computer will either not accept it or will send a "beep" and a brief message describing the difficulty. In most cases the messages will be self-explanatory and simply give you the opportunity to re-enter corrected data values.

CHAPTER 2

LINEAR PROGRAMMING

Linear programming is one of the most widely used quantitative approaches to decision making. Studies have indicated that most large corporations make at least some use of linear programming. Applications are numerous. Linear programming has been used to assist in production scheduling, choose a portfolio that will maximize return subject to constraints on risk, solve a variety of resource allocation problems, and so on.

A linear programming problem is a mathematical model of a decision-making problem that can be solved to assist a manager in making better decisions. The mathematical model is called a linear program because it consists of a linear objective function and a set of linear constraints. Solving the linear program means to optimize (maximize or minimize) the objective function subject to the limitations and requirements represented by the constraints.

To use a linear programming approach, a mathematical model that describes the objective function of the problem as well as the constraints must be formulated. Once this linear program has been developed, the Linear Programming module of *The Management Scientist* can be used to find the optimal solution.

2.1 OVERVIEW

The Linear Programming module uses the revised simplex method with LU decomposition to solve linear programs containing up to 100 variables and 50 constraints.

Significant features available with this module include:

1. The use of variable names of up to eight characters in length.

2. An on-screen editing capability that simplifies modifying problem coefficients, adding and deleting variables, and so on.

3. A standard output that includes the optimal solution as well as sensitivity analysis information. Dual prices and ranges for the objective function coefficients and right-hand sides are provided.

4. Easy-to-use menus that simplify solving linear programming problems for beginning students but still provide extensive problem-solving capabilities for more experienced users.

5. The ability to save and retrieve problems from any disk drive and subdirectory; when the user asks to retrieve a problem, a list of all previously saved problems is displayed.

6. An extensive error checking capability that prevents the user from getting "hung up" because of an error in input.

2.2   AN EXAMPLE PROBLEM

Par, Inc., is a small manufacturer of golf equipment and supplies concerned with developing a quarterly production plan for its standard and deluxe golf bags. A careful analysis of manufacturing requirements resulted in Table 2.1, which shows the production time requirements for the four manufacturing operations and the accounting department's estimate of the profit contribution per bag.

The director of manufacturing estimates that 630 hours of cutting and dyeing time, 600 hours of sewing time, 708 hours of finishing time, and 135 hours of inspection and packaging time will be available for the production of golf bags during the next three months. Par's problem is to determine how many standard and how many deluxe bags should be produced in order to maximize profit contribution.

Letting X_1 = number of standard bags Par, Inc., produces and X_2 = number of deluxe bags Par, Inc., produces, the following mathematical model can be used to find the combination of X_1 and X_2 that satisfies all the constraints and, at the same time, yields a value for the objective function that is greater than or equal to the value given by any other feasible solution.

| | **Production Time (Hours)** | | | | **Profit** |
Product	Cutting and Dyeing	Sewing	Finishing	Inspection and Packaging	**per Bag**
Standard	7/10	1/2	1	1/10	$10
Deluxe	1	5/6	2/3	1/4	$9

Table 2.1   Production Requirements and Profit Contributions per Bag

$$\max 10X_1 + 9X_2$$

s.t.

$$7/10X_1 + 1X_2 \leq 630 \quad \text{Cutting and Dyeing}$$

$$1/2X_1 + 5/6X_2 \leq 600 \quad \text{Sewing}$$

$$1X_1 + 2/3X_2 \leq 708 \quad \text{Finishing}$$

$$1/10X_1 + 1/4X_2 \leq 135 \quad \text{Inspection/Packaging}$$

$$X_1, X_2 \geq 0$$

2.3   CREATING AND SOLVING A PROBLEM

To solve the Par, Inc., problem, we begin by selecting the Linear Programming module and choosing New from the File menu; the Problem Features dialog box will then appear. Figure 2.1 shows the Problem Features dialog box after entering 2 for the Number of Decision Variables, 4 for the Number of Constraints, and choosing Maximize for the Optimization Type. After selecting OK, we obtain the data input screen shown in Figure 2.2. Note that the two decision variables have initially been given the names X1 and X2, and that the four constraints are labeled Constraint 1, Constraint 2, Constraint 3, and Constraint 4.

   After entering the objective function coefficients, the constraint coefficients, the constraint relationships, and the right-hand side values, the data input screen appears as shown in Figure 2.3. All fractional coefficients must be converted to their decimal equivalent. For

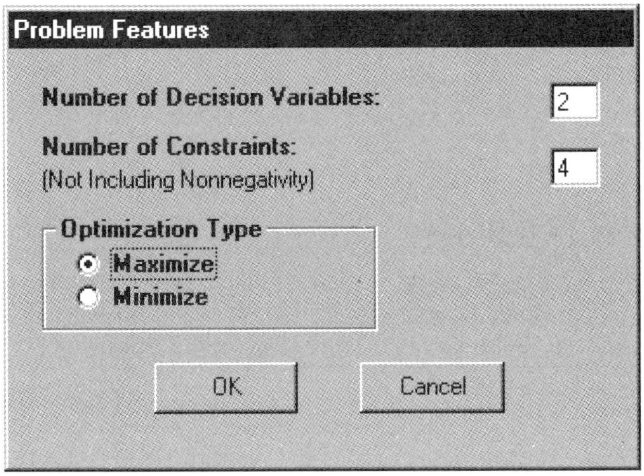

Figure 2.1   Problem Features Dialog Box

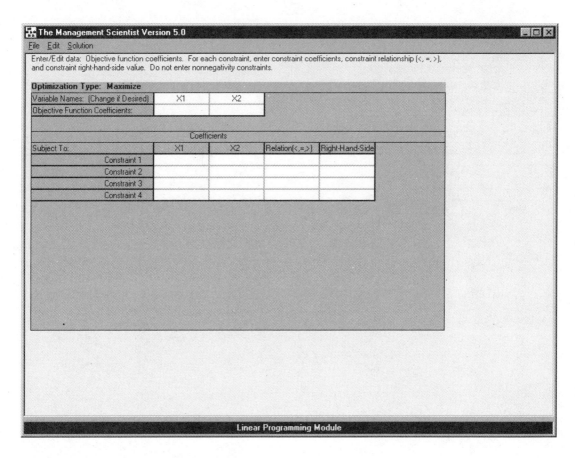

Figure 2.2   Initial Data Input Screen

example, the coefficient of X1 in the cutting and dyeing constraint must be written as .7 instead of 7/10, the coefficient of X1 in the sewing constraint must be written as .5 instead of 1/2, and so on. When rounding is necessary, we recommend using the closest five-place decimal value; thus, the 5/6 coefficient of X2 in the sewing constraint is written as .83333. Note also that each of the four less-than-or-equal-to constraints is entered using < instead of ≤, and the nonnegativity constraints, X1, X2≥0 do not have to be entered. After choosing Solve from the Solution menu, the optimal solution will be presented as shown in Figure 2.4.

2.4   INTERPRETATION OF SOLUTION

First, note the number 7667.99417, which appears to the right of the heading "Objective Function Value =." Rounding this value, we can conclude that the optimal solution to the Par, Inc., problem will provide a profit of $7668. Directly below the objective function

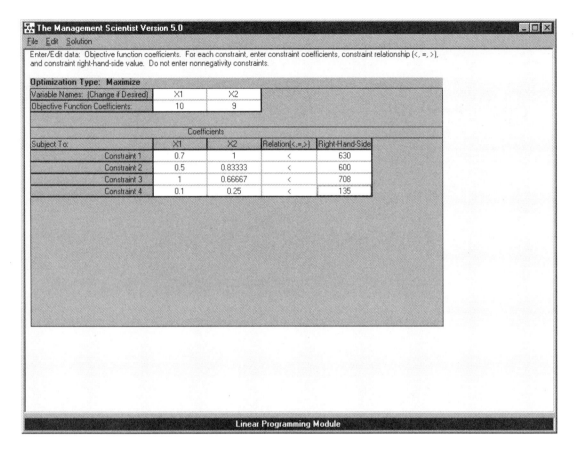

Figure 2.3   Data Input Screen for the Par, Inc., Problem

value we find the values of the decision variables in the optimal solution. After rounding, we have $X_1 = 540$ standard bags and $X_2 = 252$ deluxe bags as the optimal production quantities.

The information in the column labeled "Reduced Costs" indicates how much the objective function coefficient of each decision variable would have to improve[1] before it would be possible for that variable to assume a positive value in the optimal solution. Thus, if a decision variable is already positive—as is the case for both X_1 and X_2 in the Par, Inc., problem—its reduced cost is zero.

Immediately following the optimal X1 and X2 values and the reduced cost information, the computer output provides information about the status of the constraints. Since the Par, Inc., constraints are all of the less-than-or-equal-to type, the information shown in

---

1 For a maximization problem, improve means get bigger; for a minimization problem, improve means get smaller.

```
Objective Function Value =            7667.99417

          Variable              Value           Reduced Costs
      - - - - - - - - - - -    - - - - - - - -    - - - - - - - -
            X1               539.99842            0.00000
            X2               252.00110            0.00000

         Constraint        Slack/Surplus          Dual Prices
      - - - - - - - - - - -    - - - - - - - -    - - - - - - - -
             1                 0.00000              4.37496
             2               120.00071              0.00000
             3                 0.00000              6.93753
             4                17.99988              0.00000
```

OBJECTIVE COEFFICIENT RANGES

Variable	Lower Limit	Current Value	Upper Limit
X1	6.30000	10.00000	13.49993
X2	6.66670	9.00000	14.28571

RIGHT HAND SIDE RANGES

Constraint	Lower Limit	Current Value	Upper Limit
1	495.60000	630.00000	682.36316
2	479.99929	600.00000	No Upper Limit
3	580.00140	708.00000	900.00000
4	117.00012	135.00000	No Upper Limit

Figure 2.4 Optimal Solution to Par, Inc., Problem

the column labeled "Slack/Surplus" provides the value of the slack variable for each of the four constraints. This information is rounded and summarized below:

Constraint	Slack
1	0
2	120
3	0
4	18

From the above information we see that the binding constraints (cutting and dyeing and finishing constraints) have zero slack, or unused capacity, the sewing department has 120 hours of unused capacity, and the inspection and packaging department has 18 hours of slack, or unused capacity.

The column in Figure 2.4 labeled "Dual Prices" contains information about the marginal value of each of the four resources (time available in each department) at the optimal solution. For *The Management Scientist* the dual price is defined as follows:

The dual price associated with a constraint is the improvement in the optimal value of the objective function per unit increase in the right-hand side of the constraint.

Thus, the nonzero dual price of 4.37 for constraint 1 (cutting and dyeing) and 6.94 for constraint 3 (finishing) tell us that an additional hour of cutting and dyeing time will improve (increase) the value of the objective function by \$4.37 and an additional hour of finishing time will improve (increase) the value of the objective function by \$6.94. The range over which this interpretation is applicable will be discussed shortly. Thus, if the cutting and dyeing time were increased from 630 to 631 hours, with all other coefficients in the problem remaining the same, Par's profit would be increased by \$4.37 from \$7668 to \$7668 + \$4.37 = \$7672.37. Since the sewing and the inspection and packaging constraints both have slack or unused capacity available, the dual prices of zero show that additional hours of these two resources will not improve the value of the objective function.

From the information provided under the heading labeled OBJECTIVE COEFFICIENT RANGES, we see that as long as the profit contribution associated with the standard bag (currently a value of \$10) is between \$6.30 and \$13.50, the production of $X_1 = 540$ standard bags and $X_2 = 252$ deluxe bags will remain optimal. Similarly, as long as the profit contribution associated with the deluxe bags is between \$6.67 and \$14.29, the production of 540 standard bags and 252 deluxe bags will remain optimal.

The final section of the computer output (RIGHT HAND SIDE RANGES) contains ranging information for the constraint right-hand sides. As long as the constraint right-hand-side value stays within this range, the associated dual price gives the improvement in value of the objective function per unit increase in the right-hand side. For example, since the dual price for constraint 1 (cutting and dyeing) is \$4.37, we can conclude that additional hours will increase the objective function by \$4.37 per hour until the number of hours available reaches 682.36. It is also true that a reduction in the hours available will reduce the value of the objective function by \$4.37 per hour. From the ranging information given we see that the dual price of \$4.37 is valid as long as the right-hand-side value is between 495.60 and 682.36. For constraint 3 (finishing) we see that the dual price of \$6.94 is applicable as long as the right-hand-side value is between 580 and 900.

At this point it is important to note that the sensitivity analysis (dual prices and ranging information) presented in the computer output is based on the assumption that coefficients are changed one at a time, with all other coefficients of the problem remaining as stated in the original problem. The sensitivity analysis information provided in the computer output does not apply to two or more simultaneous changes in problem coefficients.

2.5   OTHER CONSIDERATIONS

As you solve more linear programming problems you will find that in many cases only a few of the variables appear in each constraint (i.e., they have coefficients of 0 in many constraints). *The Management Scientist* does not require you to enter any terms that have 0 coefficients. This can substantially reduce the time needed to enter a large problem.

It is often desirable to use more descriptive names for the decision variables. For example, in the Par, Inc., problem, if you wanted to use the name STANDARD instead of X1 and the name DELUXE instead of X2, you enter the name STANDARD in the X1 variable names cell and DELUXE in the X2 variable names cell. Variable names are restricted to any combination of up to eight letters or numbers; the first character, however, must be a letter.

When entering coefficients that are 1000 or greater, do *not* enter any commas. For example, a constraint that required the variable named FUNDSINV to be less than or equal to $100,000 would be written as

$$FUNDSINV \quad < \quad 100000$$

Note also that the $ symbol must be deleted when writing the right-hand-side value.

When you enter a constraint make sure that no variables appear on the right-hand side of the constraint. For example, if you have the constraint

$$VARONE = VARTWO + 10$$

you must enter this constraint as

$$VARONE - VARTWO = 10$$

Only a nonnegative numerical value may be used on the right-hand side of a constraint.

CHAPTER 3

TRANSPORTATION PROBLEM

The transportation problem arises frequently in planning for the distribution of goods and services from several supply locations to several demand locations. Usually the amount of goods available at each supply location *(origin) is* given and there is a specified amount needed at each demand location *(destination).* With a variety of shipping routes and differing costs for the routes, the objective is to determine how many units should be shipped from each origin to each destination so that all destination demands are satisfied and total transportation costs are minimized. Other applications of the transportation problem involve multiperiod production and inventory scheduling, cash management, and a variety of network flow problems.

3.1   OVERVIEW

The Transportation module of *The Management Scientist* will find the optimal solution to transportation problems with up to 30 origins and 30 destinations. The following input data must be entered by the user:

1. The number of origins.

2. The number of destinations.

3. The amount of supply at each origin.

4. The amount of demand at each destination.

5. The per unit cost or the per unit revenue of shipping from each origin to each destination.

3.2   AN EXAMPLE PROBLEM

Foster Generators, Inc., produces a particular type of generator at plants located in Cleveland, Ohio; Bedford, Indiana; and York, Pennsylvania. Production capacities for these plants over the next three-month planning period are as follows:

Origin	Plant	Three-Month Production Capacity (Units)
1	Cleveland	5000
2	Bedford	6000
3	York	2500

The firm distributes its generators through four regional distribution centers located in Boston, Chicago, St. Louis, and Lexington; the three-month forecast of demand at each distribution center is shown below:

Destination	Distribution Center	Three-Month Demand Forecast (Units)
1	Boston	6000
2	Chicago	4000
3	St. Louis	2000
4	Lexington	1500

Management would like to determine the number of units to ship from each plant to each distribution center. Since the production costs are the same at each plant, the only variable costs involved are transportation costs. Thus the problem becomes one of determining the distribution routes to be used and the quantity to be shipped via each route so that all distribution center demands can be met with a minimum total transportation cost. The cost for each unit shipped on each route is given in Table 3.1.

3.3   CREATING AND SOLVING A PROBLEM

To solve the Foster Generators' transportation problem, we begin by selecting the Transportation module and choosing New from the File menu; the Origins and Destinations dialog box will then appear. Figure 3.1 shows this dialog box after entering 3 for the number of origins and 4 for the number of destinations. After selecting OK, we ob-

	Destination			
Origin	Boston	Chicago	St. Louis	Lexington
Cleveland	3	2	7	6
Bedford	7	5	2	3
York	2	5	4	5

Table 3.1   Transportation Cost per Unit for the Foster Generators Problem

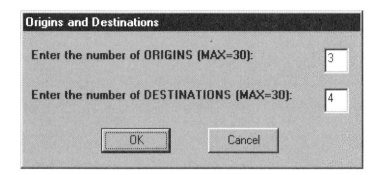

Figure 3.1   Origins and Destinations Dialog Box

tain the Transportation Tableau data input screen shown in Figure 3.2. Transportation cost per unit data from Table 3.1 are entered into the corresponding cells of the Transportation Tableau. For example, Figure 3.2 shows a cost of $3 per unit for the origin 1 (Cleveland) to destination 1 (Boston) cell, $2 per unit for origin 1 (Cleveland) to destination 2 (Chicago), and so on. After the cost per unit data are entered, the origin supplies are entered in the right-hand column of the tableau and destination demands are entered in the bottom row of the tableau. When the data input process is complete, choosing Solve from the Solution menu provides a Select Optimization Criteria dialog box where the user may specify whether a maximization objective or minimization objective is desired. Selecting minimization for the Foster Generators and selecting OK provides the optimal transportation solution as shown in Figure 3.3. Recalling the following origin and destination numbers,

Origins	**Destinations**
1. Cleveland	1. Boston
2. Bedford	2. Chicago
3. York	3. St. Louis
	4. Lexington

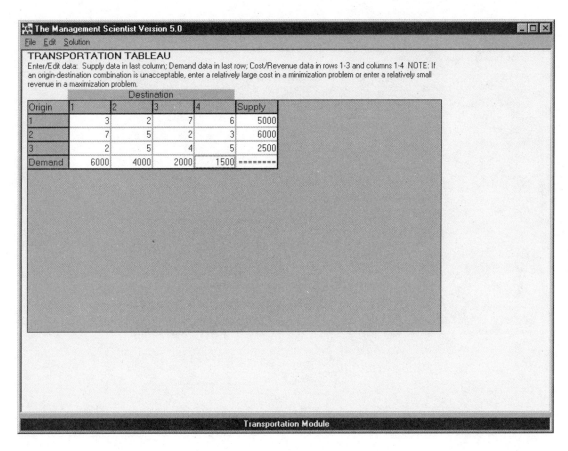

Figure 3.2   Transportation Tableau Data Input Screen

the minimum cost solution calls for shipping 3500 units from Cleveland to Boston, 1500 units from Cleveland to Chicago, 2500 units from Bedford to Chicago, 2000 units from Bedford to St. Louis, 1500 units from Bedford to Lexington, and 2500 units from York to Boston. The total transportation cost of this solution is shown to be $39,500.

3.4   OTHER CONSIDERATIONS

When supply is not equal to demand, the Transportation module recognizes the condition automatically. If supply is greater than demand, the solution will indicate which origins have excess supply. If demand exceeds supply, the program will find the best solution for the existing supply; the destinations having unsatisfied demand are then displayed.

If there are origin–destination combinations that are unacceptable, you must still enter a cost or revenue for each unacceptable combination. To ensure that these unacceptable

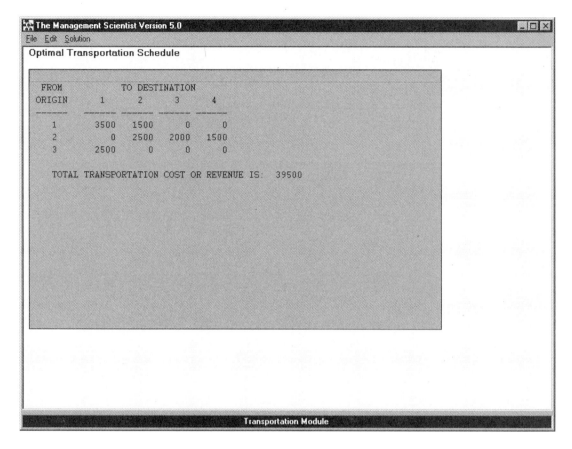

Figure 3.3   Solution Screen for the Foster Generators' Problem

transportation routes are not included in the optimal solution, enter a very large cost (e.g., 999999) or a very small revenue (e.g., –999999) where appropriate.

The Transportation module provides the capability to add or delete origins and to add or delete destinations to an existing transportation problem. Use the Edit menu to select the desired Add/Delete Origins or Destinations. The Transportation Tableau will be displayed so that the cost per unit and the supply or demand data may be entered.

Finally, if the user does not enter data in one or more cells of a Transportation Tableau, *The Management Scientist* will assign 0 values to these cells. When Solve is selected, *The Management Scientist* will provide a warning message that some of the data cells have 0 entries. The user may return to the Transportation Tableau and replace the 0 entries with appropriate data or the user may solve the transportation problem with 0 entries assumed.

CHAPTER 4

ASSIGNMENT PROBLEM

The assignment problem arises in a variety of decision-making situations. Typical assignment problems involve assigning jobs to machines, assigning workers to tasks or projects, assigning sales personnel to sales territories, assigning contracts to bidders, and so on. In general terms, the assignment problem can be thought of as assigning agents to tasks. A distinguishing feature of the assignment problem is that one agent is assigned to one and only one task. The goal is to choose the set of assignments that will optimize a stated objective, such as minimize cost, minimize time, or maximize profits.

4.1   OVERVIEW

The Assignment module of *The Management Scientist* will find the optimal solution to assignment problems with up to 30 agents and/or 30 tasks. The following input data must be entered by the user:

1. The number of agents.

2. The number of tasks.

3. The cost or revenue associated with assigning each agent to each task.

4.2   AN EXAMPLE PROBLEM

Fowle Marketing Research, Inc., is faced with the problem of assigning three available project leaders (agents) to each of three new research studies (tasks). Fowle's management realizes, however, that the time required to complete each study will depend on the experience and ability of the project leader assigned to the study. Since the three studies have been judged to have approximately the same priority, the company would like to determine the assignments that will minimize the total number of days required to complete all three. If a project leader is to be assigned to one and only one client, what assignments should be made?

With three project leaders and three clients, there is a total of nine possible assignment alternatives. The alternatives and the estimated project completion times in days are summarized in Table 4.l.

4.3 CREATING AND SOLVING A PROBLEM

To solve the Fowle Marketing Research assignment problem, we begin by selecting the Assignment module and choosing New from the File menu; the Agents and Tasks dialog box will then appear. Figure 4.1 shows this dialog box after entering 3 for the number of agents and 3 for the number of tasks. After selecting OK, we obtain the Assignment Tableau data screen shown in Figure 4.2. Assignment time data from Table 4.1 are entered into the corresponding cells of the Assignment Tableau. For example, Figure 4.2 shows 10 days for the assignment of agent 1 (Terry) to task 1 (Client 1), 15 days for the assignment of agent 1 (Terry) to task 2 (Client 2), and so on. When the data input process is completed, choosing Solve from the Solution menu provides a Select Optimization Criteria dialog box where the user may specify whether a maximization objective or minimization objective is desired. Selecting minimization for the Fowle Marketing Research problem and selecting OK provides the optimal assignment solution as shown in Figure 4.3 (page 26). Thus we see Agent 1 (Terry) is assigned to Client 2, Agent 2 (Carle) is assigned to Client 3 and Agent 3 (McClymonds) is assigned to Client 1. The minimum total time required to complete all three tasks is 26 days.

4.4 OTHER CONSIDERATIONS

When the number of agents is not equal to the number of tasks, the Assignment module recognizes the condition automatically. If the number of agents is greater than the number of tasks, the solution will indicate which agents are unassigned. If the number of tasks ex-

	Client		
Project Leader	1	2	3
1 Terry	10	15	9
2 Carle	9	18	5
3 McClymonds	6	14	3

Table 4.1 Estimated Project Completion Times (Days) for the Fowle Assignment Problem

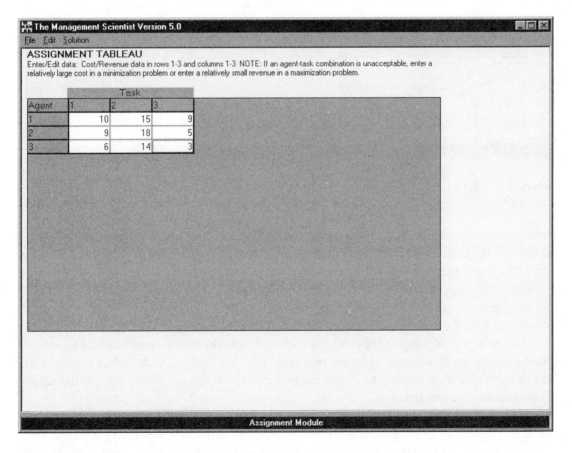

Figure 4.1   Agents and Tasks Dialog Box

Figure 4.2   Assignment Tableau Input Screen

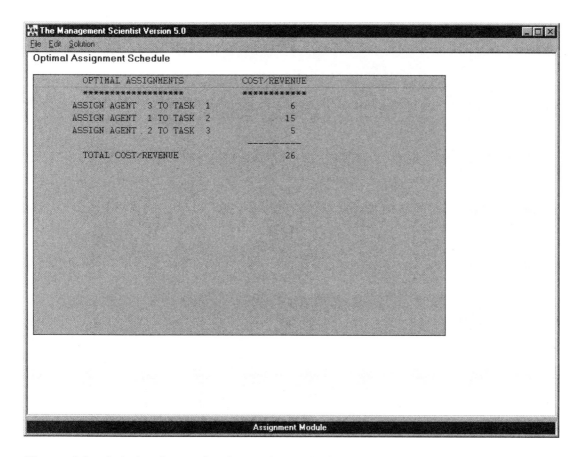

Figure 4.3   Solution Screen for the Fowle Marketing Research Program

ceeds the number of agents, the Assignment module finds the best solution for the existing agents; the tasks that are not assigned an agent are then displayed.

If there are agent–task combinations that are unacceptable, you must still enter a cost or revenue for each unacceptable agent–task combination. To ensure that these unacceptable assignments are *not* included in the optimal solution, enter a very large cost (e.g., 999999) or a very small revenue (e.g., –999999) where appropriate.

The Assignment module provides the capability to add or delete agents and to add or delete tasks to an existing assignment problem. Use the Edit menu to select the desired Add/Delete Agents or Tasks. The Assignment Tableau will be displayed so that the additional data may be entered.

Finally, if the user does not enter data in one or more cells of an Assignment Tableau, *The Management Scientist* will assign 0 values to these cells. When Solve is selected, *The Management Scientist* will provide a warning message that some of the data cells have 0 entries. The user may return to the Assignment Tableau and replace the 0 entries with appropriate data or the user may solve the assignment problem with the 0 entries assumed.

CHAPTER 5

INTEGER LINEAR PROGRAMMING

Problems that can be modeled as linear programs, except for the additional requirement that some or all of the variables must be integers, are called integer linear programming problems. The use of integer variables provides additional modeling flexibility. As a result, the number of practical applications that can be addressed with integer linear programming methodology is quite large.

If all of the variables are required to be integers, we say we have an all-integer linear program. For example, the following is an all-integer linear programming model:

$$\max 2X_1 + 3X_2$$

s.t.

$$
\begin{aligned}
3X_1 + 3X_2 &\leq 12 \\
2/3X_1 + 1X_2 &\leq 4 \\
1X_1 + 2X_2 &\leq 6 \\
X_1, X_2 &\geq 0 \text{ and integer}
\end{aligned}
$$

Note that if the phrase "and integer" is dropped from the above model we are left with the familiar two-variable linear program.

If some, but not all, of the variables in a problem are required to be integers, we say we have a mixed-integer linear program. For example, in the above model if the phrase "and integer" is replaced by "and X_2 integer" we would have a mixed-integer linear program. In this case although X_2 would be restricted to only integer values, X_1 would be said to be continuous; it could assume any value greater-than-or-equal-to zero.

In most practical applications, the integer variables are only permitted to assume the values 0 or 1. In such cases, we say that we have a binary, or a 0–1, integer linear program. Zero–one problems may be either the all-integer or mixed-integer type.

5.1   OVERVIEW

The Integer Linear Programming module of *The Management Scientist* employs a branch and bound solution procedure. It can solve all-integer, mixed-integer, and 0–1 integer linear programs with up to 100 variables and 50 constraints. However, problems with large numbers of integer variables may solve slowly. Just as with the Linear Programming module, the number of decision variables that can be used must allow for slack, surplus, and artificial variables that are added automatically by the Integer Linear Programming module.

Since the Linear Programming module and the Integer Linear Programming module are the same with respect to creating, retrieving, saving, and editing a problem, we will focus our attention on the differences associated with solving integer linear programs. Readers unfamiliar with the Linear Programming Module of *The Management Scientist* should review Chapter 2 before continuing with this chapter.

5.2   AN EXAMPLE PROBLEM:
THE ALL-INTEGER CASE

Security Realty Investors currently has $1,365,000 available to purchase townhouses or apartment buildings. The townhouses can be purchased in blocks of three for the price of $195,000 per block, but there are only four blocks of townhouses available for purchase at this time. Each building in the apartment complex sells for $237,000, and the developer has agreed to build as many units as Security would like to purchase.

Security's property manager is free to devote 140 hours per month to these investments. Each block of townhouses will require 4 hours of the property manager's time each month, while each apartment building will require 40 hours per month. The yearly cash flow (after deducting mortgage payments and operating expenses) is estimated at $2000 per block of townhouses and $3000 per apartment building. Security would like to allocate its investment funds to townhouses and apartment buildings in order to maximize the yearly cash flow.

To develop an appropriate mathematical model, let us introduce the following decision variables:

$$X_1 = \text{number of blocks of townhouses purchased}$$

$$X_2 = \text{number of apartment buildings purchased}$$

The objective function, measuring cash flow in thousands of dollars, can be written as

$$\max 2X_1 + 3X_2$$

There are three constraints that must be satisfied:

$$195X_1 + 273X_2 \leq 1365 \quad \text{Funds available (\$1000s)}$$
$$4X_1 + 40X_2 \leq 140 \quad \text{Manager's time (hours)}$$
$$X_1 \leq 4 \quad \text{Townhouses available}$$

Adding the nonnegativity requirements we obtain a linear programming model involving the two variables and three constraints. This model could be solved using the Linear Programming module described in Chapter 2; the optimal linear programming solution is $X_1 = 2.442$ and $X_2 = 3.256$, with an objective function value of 14.651.

However, since fractional values do not make any sense in the context of the problem, the standard linear programming approach to this problem is not appropriate. What we need to do is add the requirement that both X_1 and X_2 are restricted to integer values. Doing this, we obtain the following all-integer linear programming model:

$$\max 2X_1 + 3X_2$$

s.t.

$$195X_1 + 273X_2 \leq 1365 \quad \text{Funds available (\$1000s)}$$
$$4X_1 + 40X_2 \leq 140 \quad \text{Manager's time (hours)}$$
$$X_1 \leq 4 \quad \text{Townhouses available}$$
$$X_1, X_2 \geq 0 \text{ and integer}$$

5.3   CREATING AND SOLVING A PROBLEM

To solve the Security Realty Investors problem, we begin by selecting the Integer Linear Programming module and choosing New from the File menu; the Problem Features dialog box will then appear. Figure 5.1 shows the Problem Features Dialog box after entering 2 for the Number of Decision Variables, 3 for the Number of Constraints, and choosing Maximize for the Optimization Type. After selecting OK, we obtain the data input screen shown in Figure 5.2. Note that the two decision variables have initially been given the names X1 and X2, and that the three constraints are labeled Constraint 1, Constraint 2, and Constraint 3.

After entering the objective function coefficients, the constraint coefficients, the constraint relationships, and the right-hand-side values, we obtain the data input screen shown in Figure 5.3. Note that each of the three less-than-or-equal-to constraints is entered using < instead of ≤, and the nonnegativity constraints, X1, X2 ≥ 0, do *not* have to be entered. After choosing Solve from the Solution menu, we obtain the Integer Variable Identification dialog box shown in Figure 5.4 (page 32). After selecting the All Variables Are General Integer option and choosing Solve, the optimal solution will be presented as shown in Figure 5.5 (page 33).

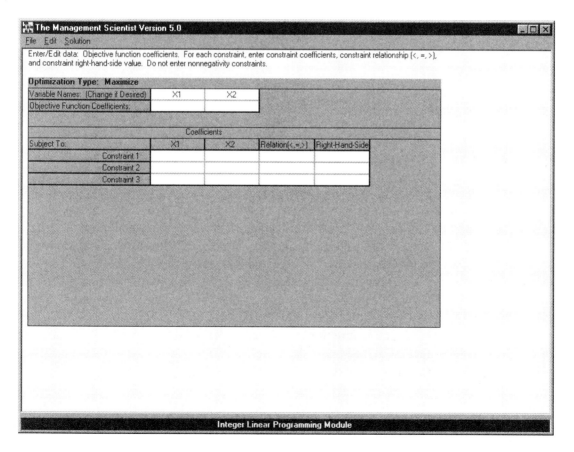

Figure 5.1   Problem Features Dialog Box

Figure 5.2   Initial Data Input Screen

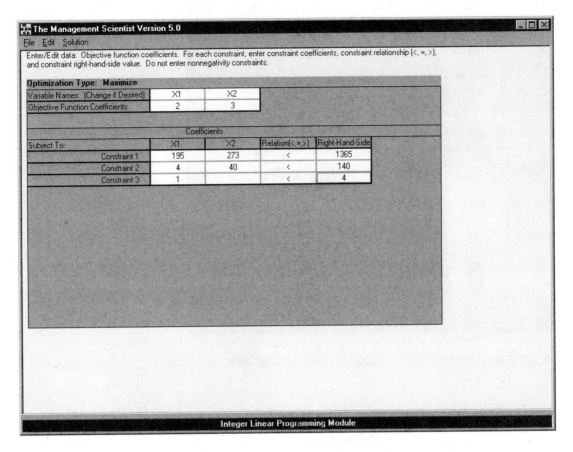

Figure 5.3   Data Input Screen for the Security Realty Investors Problem

We see that the optimal solution for Security Realty is to purchase four blocks of townhouses ($X1 = 4$) and two apartment buildings ($X2 = 2$); this solution corresponds to a yearly cash flow of $14,000.

Note that the form of the optimal solution output is similar to that of the Linear Programming module. However, the reduced costs and dual prices are not given. This is because they do not have the same meaning as for linear programming problems. Also, no ranging information is given for objective function coefficients and right-hand sides. Such information is not meaningful for integer linear programs.

5.4   AN EXAMPLE PROBLEM:
THE 0–1 ALL-INTEGER CASE

The Ice-Cold Refrigerator Company can invest funds over the next four years in a variety of company projects that have differing capital requirements. Faced with limited funds, the

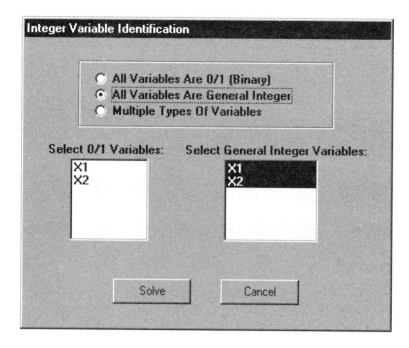

Figure 5.4   Integer Variable Identification Dialog Box

company must select the most profitable projects and budget for the necessary capital expenditures. The estimated present values for the projects, the capital requirements, and the available capital projections are as follows:

Project	Estimated Present Value($)	Capital Requirements			
		Year 1	Year 2	Year 3	Year 4
Plant expansion	90,000	15,000	20,000	20,000	15,000
Warehouse expansion	40,000	10,000	15,000	20,000	5,000
New machinery	10,000	10,000	0	0	4,000
New product research	37,000	15,000	10,000	10,000	10,000
Available capital funds		40,000	50,000	40,000	35,000

The following decision variable definitions are used:

$$X_1 = \begin{cases} 1 \text{ if the plant expansion project is accepted;} \\ 0 \text{ if rejected} \end{cases}$$

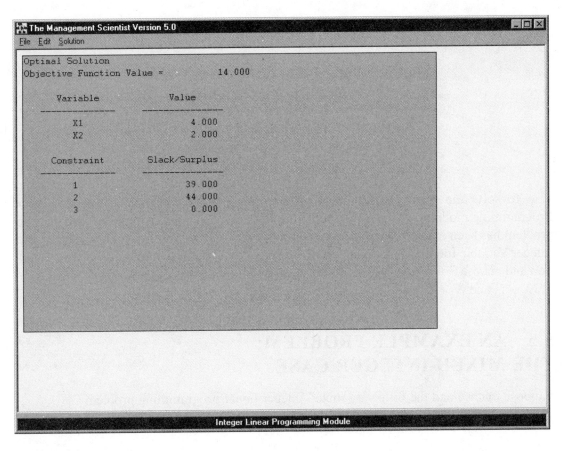

Figure 5.5   Optimal Solution to the Security Realty Problem

$$X_2 = \begin{cases} 1 \text{ if the warehouse expansion project is accepted;} \\ 0 \text{ if rejected} \end{cases}$$

$$X_3 = \begin{cases} 1 \text{ if the new machinery project is accepted;} \\ 0 \text{ if rejected} \end{cases}$$

$$X_4 = \begin{cases} 1 \text{ if the new product research project is accepted;} \\ 0 \text{ if rejected} \end{cases}$$

Using these decision variable definitions, the objective function can be written as shown below (monetary values are expressed in thousands of dollars):

$$\max 90X_1 + 40X_2 + 10X_3 + 37X_4$$

The mathematical model of this capital budgeting problem has a separate constraint for each year's available funds; thus we obtain the following four constraints:

$$15X_1 + 10X_2 + 10X_3 + 15X_4 \leq 40$$
$$20X_1 + 15X_2 \qquad\qquad\; 10X_4 \leq 50$$
$$20X_1 + 20X_2 \qquad\qquad\; 10X_4 \leq 40$$
$$15X_1 + 5X_2 + 4X_3 + 10X_4 \leq 35$$
$$X_1, X_2, X_3, X_4 = 0,1$$

To solve the above integer linear programming problem using the Integer Linear Programming module, we enter the problem in the usual fashion. After verifying that the problem has been entered correctly, we choose Solve from the Solution menu. Then, in the Integer Variable Identification dialog box, we select the All Variables Are 0/1 (Binary) option and choose Solve; the optimal solution, shown in Figure 5.6, is given by $X_1 = 1$, $X_2 = 1$, $X_3 = 1$, and $X_4 = 0$ with a total estimated present value of $140,000.

5.5 AN EXAMPLE PROBLEM: THE MIXED-INTEGER CASE

Suppose that we had the following mixed-integer linear programming problem:

$$\max 1X_1 + 1X_2$$
$$\text{s.t.}$$
$$7X_1 + 9X_2 \leq 63$$
$$9X_1 + 5X_2 \leq 45$$
$$3X_1 + 1X_2 \leq 12$$
$$X_1, X_2 \geq 0 \text{ and } X_2 \text{ integer}$$

After entering this problem, we choose Solve from the Solution menu. Then, in the Integer Variable Identification dialog box we select the Multiple Types of Variables option. From the General Integer Variables list we choose X2.

After selecting Solve, the optimal mixed integer solution is displayed as shown in Figure 5.7.

5.6 OTHER CONSIDERATIONS

The Integer Linear Programming module of *The Management Scientist* is a general integer programming system; that is, it has the capability of solving every type of integer linear

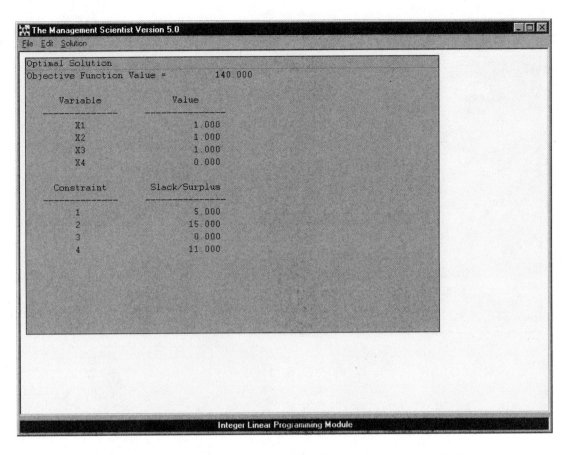

Figure 5.6   Optimal Solution to the Ice-Cold Refrigerator Company Problem

programming problem. A branch and bound solution procedure, which requires the solution of a linear programming problem at each node, is employed. The number of computations involved in solving these problems can be substantial for even moderately sized problems. Thus, solution times may take as long as several minutes for more difficult problems and will depend on the speed of your personal computer.

Sensitivity analysis is often more critical for integer linear programming problems than for linear programming problems. A very small change in one of the coefficients in the constraints can cause a relatively large change in the value of the optimal solution. But, the dual prices and ranging information made available with the solution of linear programming problems are not helpful with integer linear programming problems. Thus, practitioners usually recommend resolving an integer linear program several times with slight variations in the coefficients to explore sensitivity issues before attempting to choose an optimal solution for implementation.

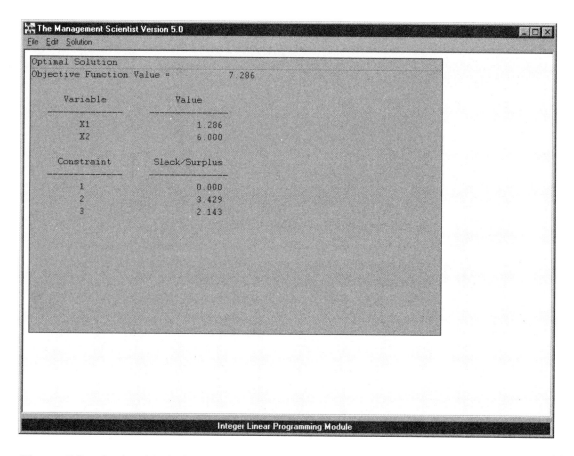

Figure 5.7   Optimal Solution to the Mixed-Integer Example Problem

CHAPTER 6

SHORTEST ROUTE

In this chapter, we consider the network application of designing a transportation system where the primary interest is in determining the shortest route or shortest path through the network. These types of problems arise in situations where it is desired to transport goods between a variety of locations and the objective is to find the most economical route between various pairs of locations.

The cost of transporting goods from one location to another is usually measured in distance traveled, but travel time or dollar cost could be used just as easily. Other situations in which the need to solve a shortest route problem might arise, include the design of computer networks, vehicle routing problems, and so on.

6.1   OVERVIEW

The Shortest Route module of *The Management Scientist* will find the shortest distance between any 2 nodes in a network consisting of up to 20 nodes and 40 arcs. To create and solve a new problem, the user must first develop a network diagram of the problem to be solved and then provide the following data input to the Shortest Route module:

1. The number of nodes

2. The number of arcs

3. For each arc:
   a. The number of the start node
   b. The number of the end node
   c. The distance (or other measure used) between the nodes
4. The 2 nodes it is desired to find the shortest route between

6.2   AN EXAMPLE PROBLEM

The Gorman Construction Company operates several construction projects located throughout a three-county area. With multiple daily trips carrying personnel, equipment, and supplies to and from the construction sites, the costs associated with transportation activities are substantial. The network shown in Figure 6.1 describes the travel alternatives to and from six of Gorman's newest construction sites. The circles (nodes) of the network correspond to the site locations. The lines between the nodes (arcs) correspond to the roads and the streets between the locations. The numbers next to each arc represent road distances in miles. If Gorman wishes to minimize the travel distance from the office to site 7, what is the route that should be followed? Note that the network has 7 nodes and 10 arcs.

6.3   CREATING AND SOLVING A PROBLEM

To solve the Gorman shortest route problem, we begin by selecting the Shortest Route module and choosing New from the File menu; the Nodes and Arcs dialog box will then appear. Figure 6.2 shows this dialog box after entering 7 for the number of nodes and 10 for the number of arcs. After selecting OK, we obtain the Network Description data input screen shown in Figure 6.3. Network description data are entered into the corresponding cells. For example, row 1 corresponds to arc 1 of the network, which starts at node 1, ends at node 2, and has a distance of 15 miles. Row 2 corresponds to arc 2 of the network, which starts at node 1, ends at node 3, and has a distance of 10 miles. The numbering of the 10 arcs as shown in Figure 6.3 is arbitrary. A different user might number the arcs differently

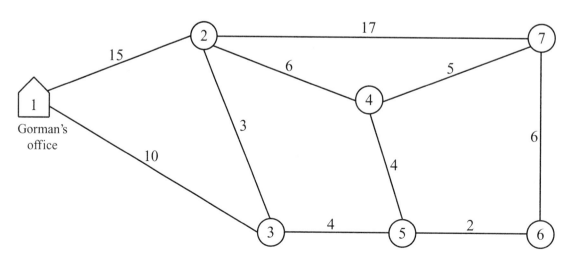

Figure 6.1   Road Network for the Gorman Shortest Route Problem

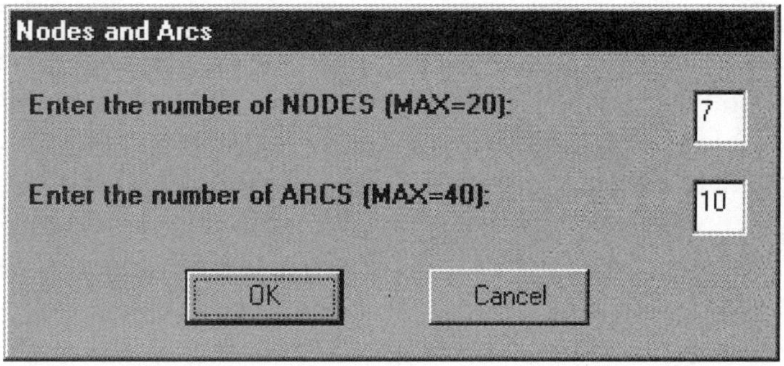

Figure 6.2 Nodes and Arcs Dialog Box

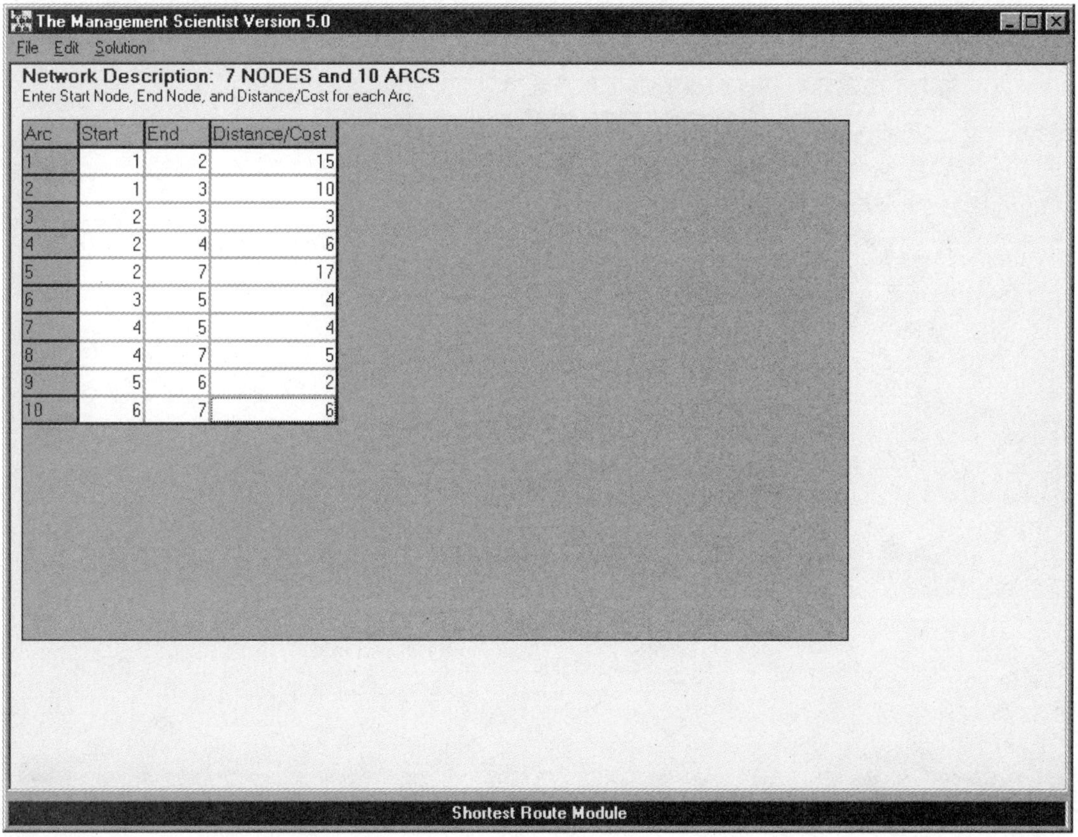

Arc	Start	End	Distance/Cost
1	1	2	15
2	1	3	10
3	2	3	3
4	2	4	6
5	2	7	17
6	3	5	4
7	4	5	4
8	4	7	5
9	5	6	2
10	6	7	6

Figure 6.3 Network Description Data Input Screen

and input the network description data in a different order. *The Management Scientist* is flexible and can accept the network arc descriptions in any order. When the data input process is completed, choosing Solve from the Solution menu provides a Select the Starting and Ending Nodes dialog box where the user may specify any starting node and any ending node in the network. Selecting starting node 1 and ending node 7 for the Gorman problem and selecting OK provides the optimal shortest route as shown in Figure 6.4. Thus we see that the shortest route between nodes 1 and 7 passes through nodes 3, 5, and 6. The total distance is 22 miles.

At this point, the user may select Solve from the Solution menu again. Altering the starting node and/or ending node and selecting OK will provide the shortest route between the two specified nodes. This process can be repeated in order to find the shortest route between any other pair of nodes in the network.

```
The Management Scientist Version 5.0                              _ □ ×
File  Edit  Solution
Optimal Route

         THE SHORTEST ROUTE FROM NODE 1 TO NODE 7
         ********************************************
         START NODE        END NODE        DISTANCE
         ----------        --------        --------
             1                 3              10
             3                 5               4
             5                 6               2
             6                 7               6
               TOTAL DISTANCE                 22




                      Shortest Route Module
```

Figure 6.4   Shortest Route Between Nodes 1 and 7 for the Gorman Problem

CHAPTER 7

MINIMAL
SPANNING TREE

The minimal spanning tree problem involves using the arcs of the network to connect all nodes in such a fashion that the total length of the arcs used is minimized. As with the shortest route problem, it is customary to use distance as a measure of arc length. However, in some applications it is more appropriate to use arc cost, time to go from one node to another, and so on.

A common situation in which the minimal spanning tree problem arises involves the design of communication networks, where the objective is to minimize the amount of the cable necessary to connect all nodes that must communicate with one another. Other applications involve designing road networks, developing the layout for conveyor systems, and so on.

7.1   OVERVIEW

The Minimal Spanning Tree module of *The Management Scientist* will find the optimal solution to minimal spanning tree problems with up to 20 nodes and 40 arcs. The module will find the set of arcs that creates a path connecting every node to every other node in such a manner that the total length of all arcs used is minimized. To create and solve a new problem, the user must first develop a network diagram of the problem to be solved and then provide the following input data:

1. The number of nodes

2. The number of arcs

3. For each arc:

   a. The number of the start node

  b. The number of the end node

  c. The distance (or other measure used) between the nodes

7.2 AN EXAMPLE PROBLEM

The Southwestern Regional Computer Center must have special computer communication lines installed in order to connect five satellite users with a new central computer. Because the lines are expensive, the computer center's management wants the total length of the new communication lines to be as small as possible. While the central computer could be connected directly to each user, it appears to be more economical to install a direct line to some users and let other users tap into the system by linking up with the users who are already connected to the system. The network shown in Figure 7.1 shows us the links being considered between the regional computer center and the satellite users. The distance, in miles, between locations is shown above the associated arcs. Note that the network has 6 nodes and 11 arcs.

7.3 CREATING AND SOLVING A PROBLEM

To solve the Regional Computer System minimal spanning tree problem, we begin by selecting the Minimal Spanning Tree module and choosing New from the File menu; the Nodes and Arcs dialog box will then appear. Figure 7.2 shows this dialog box after entering 6 for the number of nodes and 11 for the number of arcs. After selecting OK, we obtain the Network Description data input screen shown in Figure 7.3. Network description data are entered into the corresponding cells. For example, row 1 corresponds to arc 1 of the network, which starts at node 1, ends at node 2, and has a distance of 20 miles. Row 2 corresponds to arc 2 of the network, which starts at node 1, ends at node 3, and has a distance of 40 miles. The numbering of the 11 arcs as shown in Figure 7.3 is arbitrary. A different user might number the arcs differently and input the network description data in a different order. *The Management Scientist* is flexible and can accept the network arc descriptions in any order. When the data input process is completed, choosing Solve from the Solution menu provides the minimal spanning tree solution as shown in Figure 7.4 (page 45). Thus we see that communication lines must be installed between five pairs of locations: 1 and 2, 1 and 4, 4 and 3, 4 and 6, and 3 and 5. The total length of the communication lines is 110 miles.

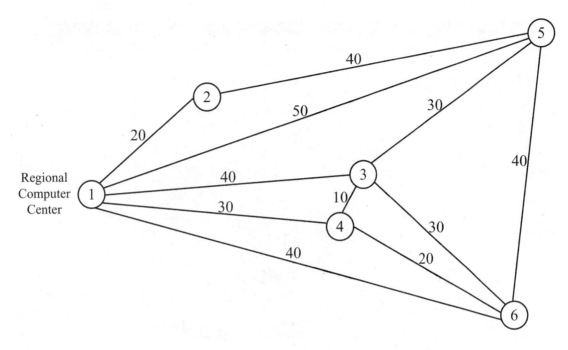

Figure 7.1 Communications Network for the Regional Computer System

Figure 7.2 Nodes and Arcs Dialog Box

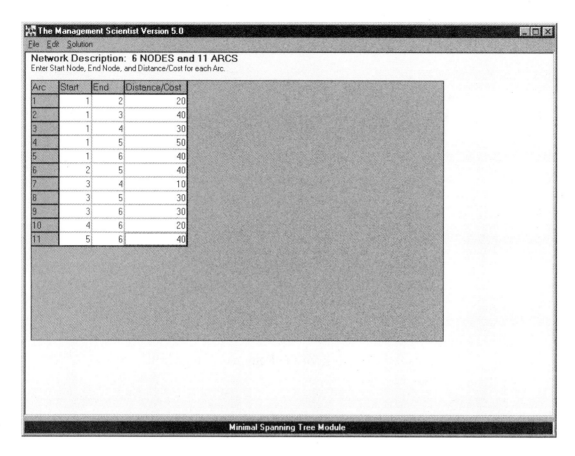

Figure 7.3 Network Description Data Input Screen

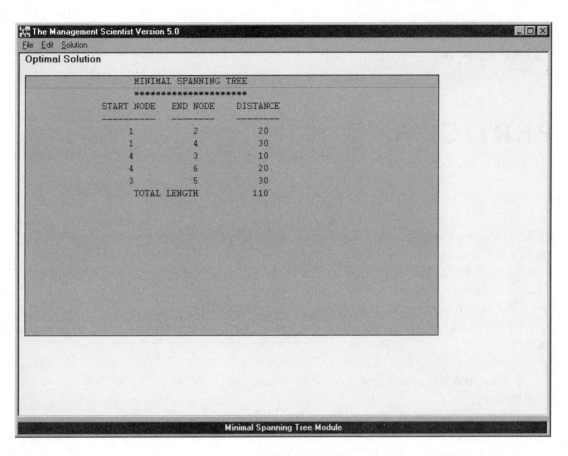

Figure 7.4   Minimal Spanning Tree for the Regional Computer Center Problem

CHAPTER 8

PERT/CPM

PERT (Program Evaluation and Review Technique) and CPM (Critical Path Method) are approaches management scientists have developed to assist managers with planning, scheduling, and controlling projects. PERT and CPM were initially developed independently for slightly different purposes, but in today's usage, the distinction between PERT and CPM as two separate techniques has largely disappeared.

PERT/CPM has been used to plan, schedule, and control a wide variety of projects, such as:

1. Research and development of new products and processes

2. Construction of plants, buildings, and highways

3. Maintenance of large and complex equipment

4. Design and installation of new systems

In projects such as the above, project managers must schedule and coordinate the various activities so that the entire project is completed on time. A complicating factor in carrying out this task is the interdependence of the activities; some activities depend on the completion of other activities before they can be started. The PERT/CPM technique can assist managers by helping them answer questions such as the following:

1. What is the time required to complete the project?

2. What start and finish dates should be scheduled for each activity?

3. Which are the critical activities?

4. How long can noncritical activities be delayed before they become critical?

8.1 OVERVIEW

The PERT/CPM module of *The Management Scientist* can be used to analyze projects with up to 25 activities. The program will develop an activity schedule, identify the critical activities, and compute the expected project completion time. It can be used for projects with known activity completion times and for projects with uncertain activity completion times. For projects with uncertain activity completion times, the PERT/CPM module will compute the expected time and variance for each activity as well as the expected completion time and variance for the entire project.

Before using the PERT/CPM module, the user must develop a list of the activities and, for each activity, the immediate predecessors. Each activity must be identified by a letter of the alphabet and *no activity may have as an immediate predecessor an activity identified by a letter coming later in the alphabet*. The data input requirements differ depending on whether activity times are known or uncertain. We illustrate the use of the module in both cases.

8.2 AN EXAMPLE PROBLEM WITH KNOWN ACTIVITY COMPLETION TIMES

The owner of the Western Hills Shopping Center is considering modernizing and expanding his current 32-store shopping complex. The activities necessary to complete the expansion project are listed in Table 8.1. Note that the list includes the immediate predecessor for each activity as well as the number of weeks required to complete the activity.

Activity	Activity Description	Immediate Predecessor	Completion Time (Weeks)
A	Prepare architectural drawings	—	5
B	Identify potential tenants	—	6
C	Develop prospectus	A	4
D	Select contractor	A	3
E	Prepare building permits	A	1
F	Secure approval of building permits	E	4
G	Construction	D, F	14
H	Finalize tenant contracts	B, C	12
I	Tenants move in	G, H	2

Table 8.1 Activity List for the Western Hills Shopping Center Expansion Project

Information in Table 8.1 indicates that the total time required to complete all activities in the shopping center expansion project is 51 weeks. However, from the immediate predecessor information, we see that several of the activities can be completed simultaneously (A and B, for example). Being able to work on two or more activities at the same time will shorten the total project completion time to less than 51 weeks. We now show how the PERT/CPM module can be used to provide information in managing this project.

8.3   CREATING AND SOLVING A PROBLEM

To analyze the Western Hills Shopping Center expansion project, we begin by selecting the PERT/CPM module and choosing New from the File menu; the PERT/CPM Parameters dialog box will then appear. Figure 8.1 shows the PERT/CPM Parameters dialog box after selecting the Known Activity Times option and entering 9 for the Number of Activities. After selecting OK, we obtain the data input screen shown in Figure 8.2.

For each of the nine activities in the Select Activity Name list we must identify each activity's immediate predecessor and the expected activity time for each activity. For example, we begin by clicking the letter A in the Select Activity Name list. Since A does not have any immediate predecessor, we only need to enter the expected completion time of 5 in the Expected Time box. The input for other activities follows in a similar fashion, with the exception that for activities with immediate predecessors, we must also choose the immediate predecessors from the Select Predecessor list. Figure 8.3 on page 50 shows the data input screen after entering all the data for the Western Hills Shopping Center expansion project. After choosing Solve from the Solution menu, the activity schedule, critical path, and project completion time will be displayed as shown in Figure 8.4 on page 51.

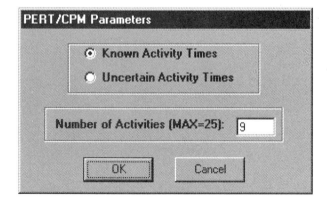

Figure 8.1   PERT/CPM Parameters Dialog Box

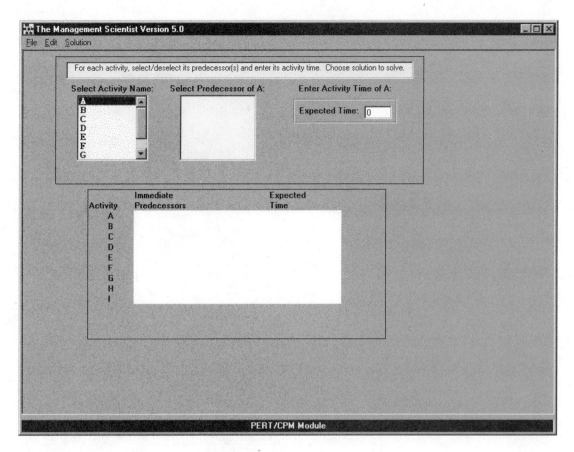

Figure 8.2   Initial Data Input Screen

Activities A–E–F–G–I are on the critical path and the project may be completed in 26 weeks. The earliest start, latest start, earliest finish, latest finish, and slack times are shown for each activity.

8.4   AN EXAMPLE PROBLEM WITH UNCERTAIN ACTIVITY COMPLETION TIMES

The H.S. Daugherty Company is considering manufacturing a cordless vacuum cleaner that can be powered by a rechargeable battery. The vacuum cleaner, referred to as a Porta-Vac, is expected to contribute to Daugherty's expansion into the household market. Daugherty's management has initiated a project to study the feasibility of proceeding with the Porta-Vac idea. The list of activities and immediate predecessors are shown in Table 8.2 on page 51.

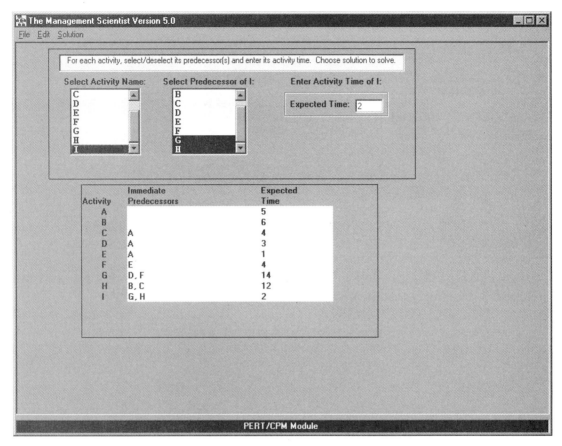

Figure 8.3   Data Input Screen for the Western Hills Shopping Center Project

For the Daugherty Porta-Vac project, activity times are uncertain. In such cases, the PERT procedure calls for three time estimates (optimistic, most probable, and pessimistic) to be used for each activity. The activity time estimates for the Porta-Vac project are given in Table 8.3.

To analyze the Daugherty Porta-Vac project using the PERT/CPM module, we begin by choosing New from the File menu. In the Enter PERT /CPM Parameters dialog box, we select the Uncertain Activity times option, enter 10 for the Number of Activities, and select OK; the problem input screen will then appear. Then, for each activity, in addition to the information on immediate predecessors, we must enter the optimistic, most probable, and pessimistic time estimates; Figure 8.5 shows the resulting problem input screen.

After choosing Solve from the Solution menu, we obtain the output shown in Figure 8.6. The PERT/CPM module prints a list of the expected times and variances for activities, followed by the activity schedule, the critical path, the expected project completion time,

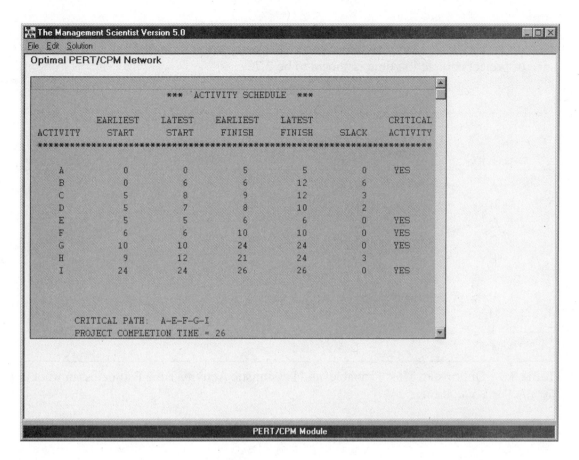

Figure 8.4   Activity Schedule for the Western Hills Shopping Center Project

Activity	Description	Immediate Predecessors
A	Develop product design	—
B	Plan market research	—
C	Routing (manufacturing engineering)	A
D	Build prototype model	A
E	Prepare marketing brochure	A
F	Cost estimates	C
G	Preliminary product testing	D
H	Market survey	B, E
I	Pricing and forecast report	H
J	Final report	F, G, I

Table 8.2   Activity List for the Daugherty Porta-Vac Project

and the variance of project completion time. For the Daugherty Porta-Vac project the critical path is A–E–H–I–J, with an expected project completion time of 17 weeks. The variance of project completion time is shown to be 2.72.

Activity	Optimistic Time	Most Probable Time	Pessimistic Time
A	4	5	12
B	1	1.5	5
C	2	3	4
D	3	4	11
E	2	3	4
F	1.5	2	2.5
G	1.5	3	4.5
H	2.5	3.5	7.5
I	1.5	2	2.5
J	1	2	3

Table 8.3   Optimistic, Most Probable, and Pessimistic Activity Time Estimates (in weeks) for the Porta-Vac Project

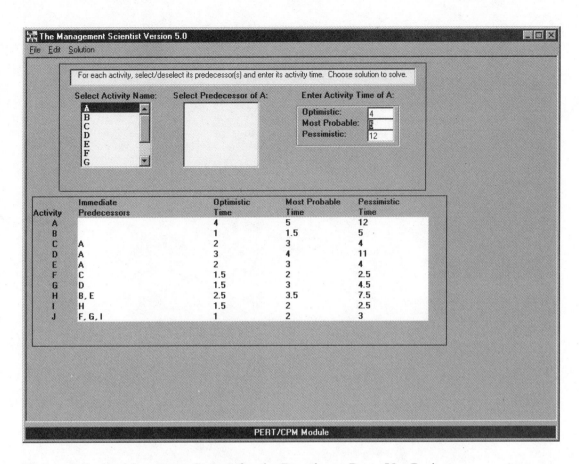

Figure 8.5 Problem Input Screen for the Daugherty Porta-Vac Project

```
┌──────────────────────────────────────────────────────────────────────────┐
│ 🎯 The Management Scientist Version 5.0                          _ ▢ ✕     │
├──────────────────────────────────────────────────────────────────────────┤
│ File  Edit  Solution                                                        │
├──────────────────────────────────────────────────────────────────────────┤
│ Optimal PERT/CPM Network                                                    │
│ ┌──────────────────────────────────────────────────────────────────┐ ▲    │
│ │           EXPECTED TIMES AND VARIANCES FOR ACTIVITIES             │ ▒    │
│ │                                                                   │      │
│ │           ACTIVITY      EXPECTED TIME      VARIANCE               │      │
│ │      ***************************************************          │      │
│ │              A               6               1.78                 │      │
│ │              B               2               0.44                 │      │
│ │              C               3               0.11                 │      │
│ │              D               5               1.78                 │      │
│ │              E               3               0.11                 │      │
│ │              F               2               0.03                 │      │
│ │              G               3               0.25                 │      │
│ │              H               4               0.69                 │      │
│ │              I               2               0.03                 │      │
│ │              J               2               0.11                 │      │
│ │      ***************************************************          │      │
│ │                                                                   │      │
│ │              ***   ACTIVITY SCHEDULE   ***                        │      │
│ │                                                                   │      │
│ │        EARLIEST    LATEST    EARLIEST    LATEST           CRITICAL│      │
│ │ ACTIVITY  START     START     FINISH     FINISH   SLACK   ACTIVITY│      │
│ │ ******************************************************************│      │
│ │                                                                   │      │
│ │     A        0         0         6          6        0     YES    │      │
│ │     B        0         7         2          9        7            │      │
│ │     C        6        10         9         13        4            │      │
│ │     D        6         7        11         12        1            │      │
│ │     E        6         6         9          9        0     YES    │      │
│ │     F        9        13        11         15        4            │      │
│ │     G       11        12        14         15        1            │      │
│ │     H        9         9        13         13        0     YES    │      │
│ │     I       13        13        15         15        0     YES    │      │
│ │     J       15        15        17         17        0     YES    │      │
│ │                                                                   │      │
│ │                                                                   │      │
│ │     CRITICAL PATH:  A-E-H-I-J                                      │      │
│ │     EXPECTED PROJECT COMPLETION TIME = 17                          │ ▒    │
│ │     VARIANCE OF PROJECT COMPLETION TIME = 2.72                     │ ▼    │
│ └──────────────────────────────────────────────────────────────────┘      │
│                                                                            │
│                                                                            │
│                              PERT/CPM Module                               │
└──────────────────────────────────────────────────────────────────────────┘
```

Figure 8.6   Activity Schedule for the Daugherty Porta-Vac Project

CHAPTER 9

INVENTORY

Inventories can be defined as any idle products or materials that are waiting to be used. For most companies, the expenses associated with financing and maintaining inventories are a substantial part of the cost of doing business.

Quantitative models of inventory systems have been developed to help managers make decisions such as the following:

1. How much should be ordered when the inventory for a particular item is to be replenished?

2. When should the inventory of the item be replenished?

In the best known and most fundamental inventory model, referred to as the economic order quantity model, the objective is to satisfy demand while minimizing inventory holding costs and ordering costs. In other inventory models, backorder costs, quantity discount costs, and stockout costs are also considered.

While there are many similarities in all inventory systems, each system has unique characteristics that prevent the application of one or two general inventory models to all situations. For example, in some inventory systems it may be reasonable to assume that demand is *deterministic*; that is, the demand for the item occurs at a known and constant rate. In other inventory systems, however, the demand may be *probabilistic*; that is, the demand fluctuates and can only be described in probabilistic terms.

Based on assumptions about the type of demand encountered and given relevant costs, inventory models can be used to provide information such as the following:

1. Minimum cost order quantity

2. Annual inventory holding cost

3. Annual order cost

4. Total annual cost

5. Maximum inventory level

6. Average inventory level

7. Reorder point

8. Number of orders per year

9. Cycle time (time between orders)

Using the information provided by an inventory model, managers are better equipped to establish a low-cost inventory policy.

9.1   OVERVIEW

The Inventory module of *The Management Scientist* provides the following six inventory models:

1. *Economic Order Quantity*—Given a constant demand rate, this model determines the order quantity that will minimize the total annual inventory holding and ordering costs.

2. *Economic Production Lot Size*—Given a constant demand rate and a constant production rate, this model determines the production lot size that will minimize the total annual inventory holding and production setup costs.

3. *Economic Order Quantity with Planned Shortages*—This model allows planned shortages or backorders. Given a constant demand rate, this model determines the order quantity that will minimize the total annual inventory holding, ordering, and backordering costs.

4. *Economic Order Quantity with Quantity Discounts*—This model considers cases where the purchase cost per unit changes depending on the order quantity. Given a constant demand rate, this model determines the order quantity that will minimize the total annual inventory holding, ordering, and purchasing costs.

5. *Order Quantity–Reorder Point with Probabilistic Demand*—This model follows the approach of the economic order quantity model with the addition that demand during the lead time period is probabilistic and described by a normal probability

distribution. The model determines the order quantity and reorder point that will minimize annual inventory holding and ordering costs and provides an acceptable value for the probability of a stockout.

6. *Single-Period Inventory with Probabilistic Demand*—With demand described by a uniform or normal probability distribution, this model determines the optimal order quantity for single-period inventory situations in which items cannot be carried in inventory from one period to the next.

9.2   AN EXAMPLE PROBLEM

R&B Beverage Company is a distributor of beer, wine, and soft drink products. For each of its products, R&B would like to determine how much to order and when to order so that inventory holding and ordering costs are minimized. To illustrate how the Inventory module can help in determining answers to these questions, we will apply the economic order quantity model to R&B's bestselling product, Bub Beer.

The annual demand for Bub Beer is assumed to be approximately constant at 104,000 cases. It costs $32.00 to place an order with the supplier, and each case of Bub costs R&B $8.00. The annual inventory holding cost per unit is 25% of the cost of the item, and the R&B Beverage Company operates 250 days per year. In addition, when a new order is placed with the supplier, it takes two days for the order to reach the R&B warehouse. Given these data regarding Bub Beer, management would like to answer the following questions:

1. What is the minimum cost order quantity of Bub Beer?

2. What is the reorder point or inventory level that signals R&B should order a new shipment of Bub Beer?

3. How many orders will be placed per year and what is the length of time between orders?

4. What is the total annual inventory holding and ordering cost for this product?

9.3   CREATING AND SOLVING A PROBLEM

To solve the Bub Beer inventory problem, we begin by selecting the Inventory module and choosing New from the File menu; the Inventory Models Available dialog box shown in Figure 9.1 will then appear. This dialog box can be used to select any one of the six inventory models listed. Since the Bub Beer problem is an economic order quantity application, we select the economic order quantity model. The dialog box shown in Figure 9.2 appears

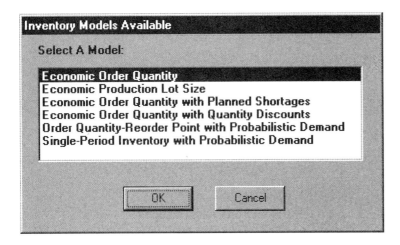

Figure 9.1 Inventory Models Available Dialog Box

on the screen. The data for the Bub Beer problem are entered as shown. Note that the Holding Cost Method shows Percent with the Percent of Unit Cost = 25 (for 25%) and Unit Cost = 8. The Holding Cost Method can be changed to Amount, which requires the user to input the holding cost amount per unit. The Percent and Amount options enable inventory

Figure 9.2 Economic Order Quantity Dialog Box

holding cost to be expressed as either a percentage of the unit cost or as a specific dollar amount. The Number of Working Days per Year will show 250 days, which is a common assumption. If 250 days per year is not appropriate, this entry can be changed to reflect the actual number of working days per year for the problem. Finally, Compute Reorder Point appears as a question since the economic order quantity model can be implemented with or without reorder point information. Since the Bub Beer problem requested reorder point information, the Compute Reorder Point box has been clicked on and the lead time of 2 days has been entered.

After the data input process is completed, Solve or Save can be implemented by selecting the appropriate button in the data input dialog box. Selecting Solve provides the optimal solution shown in Figure 9.3. Thus, we see that the economic order quantity for Bub Beer is 1824.28 units, and the reorder point is 832 units. This optimal inventory policy will result in approximately 57 orders per year with the time between orders 4.39 days. Note also that the total annual cost is $3,648.56.

```
The Management Scientist Version 5.0                                    _ □ ×
File  Edit  Solution
                          INVENTORY POLICY
                          ****************

        OPTIMAL ORDER QUANTITY                1,824.28

        ANNUAL INVENTORY HOLDING COST        $1,824.28

        ANNUAL ORDERING COST                 $1,824.28

        TOTAL ANNUAL COST                    $3,648.56

        MAXIMUM INVENTORY LEVEL               1,824.28

        AVERAGE INVENTORY LEVEL                 912.14

        REORDER POINT                           832.00

        NUMBER OF ORDERS PER YEAR                57.01

        CYCLE TIME (DAYS)                         4.39




                    Inventory Model: Economic Order Quantity
```

Figure 9.3   Output for the R&B Beverage Economic Order Quantity Problem

It is well known that the optimal order quantity provided by the economic order quantity model is not sensitive to rounding error. Thus, in practice, rounding the optimal order quantity to a more convenient quantity (such as 1800, 1900, or 2000 units) can be expected to have little effect on the total annual cost.

9.4   OTHER INVENTORY MODELS

There are six different inventory models that may be solved using this module (see Figure 9.1). The process of creating and solving a problem is similar for all the models. Here, we briefly overview the differences in data input and the output provided.

Economic Production Lot Size

This model is appropriate for problems involving a production run. It is similar to the economic order quantity model; the production lot size run corresponds to the economic order quantity and the production setup cost corresponds to an order cost. Attention is usually focused on the following questions:

1. What is the minimum cost production lot size?

2. What is the reorder point or inventory level that signals a new production run should be scheduled?

3. How many production setups will be scheduled per year and what is the length of time between production runs?

4. What is the total annual inventory holding and setup cost for this product?

Data input for the economic production lot size model is very similar to the data input for the economic order quantity model shown in Figure 9.2. One additional input item—the annual production rate—is required for the production lot size model.

Economic Order Quantity with Planned Shortages

This inventory model uses the assumption of the economic order quantity model with the exception that it allows planned shortages called *backorders*. The model assumes that if the item is out of inventory, the customer requesting the item will wait until the next incoming order is received, and such backorders will be filled as soon as the new order is received.

Data input includes the economic order quantity data input shown in Figure 9.2 plus one additional piece of information: the cost per unit per year for a backorder. Output information includes the standard economic order quantity information shown in Figure

9.3. In addition, the planned stockouts model indicates the maximum number of back-orders that will occur, the annual cost of the backorders, and the total cost including inventory holding, ordering, and backordering costs.

Economic Order Quantity with Quantity Discounts

This model is based on the economic order quantity model with the variation that purchase cost per unit is a relevant cost and depends on the order quantity decision. Thus, in this model it may be desirable to order additional units in order to obtain a quantity discount, which will result in a lower unit cost.

The economic order quantity with quantity discounts model requires the same input data as the economic order quantity model (see Figure 9.2). In addition, this model requires you to enter quantity discount information showing the unit cost and the minimum quantity to order to obtain this cost for each discount category.

The output information is the same as for the economic order quantity model as shown in Figure 9.3, with the addition that purchase cost is included in the total cost. The recommended optimal order quantity will be in the discount category providing the lowest total cost.

Order Quantity–Reorder Point with Probabilistic Demand

This inventory model is another variation of the basic economic order quantity model. The difference between the two models is that the order quantity–reorder point with probabilistic demand model assumes that demand during the lead time is subject to uncertainty. A normal probability distribution is used to describe the lead time demand.

Data input includes the basic economic order quantity data input shown in Figure 9.2, with the exception that the reorder point is based on the input of the mean and standard deviation of the lead time demand rather than on the input of lead time in days. The computation of the reorder point is made based on a desired *service level*. The service level can be expressed in terms of either

1. An allowable number of stockouts per year, or

2. The probability of a stockout during an inventory cycle.

The choice of the expression of service level is up to the user. Under option 1, the allowable number of stockouts per year is specified. Under option 2, the acceptable probability of a stockout during an inventory cycle is specified. Generally, most inventory systems will seek to have inventory available for customers and thus the allowable number of stockouts per year and the probability of a stockout per cycle will be low.

The output information displayed includes the economic order quantity model information shown in Figure 9.3. In addition the output displays the safety stock level, the safety stock cost, the expected number of stockouts per year, and the probability of a stockout per cycle.

Single-Period Inventory with Probabilistic Demand

This inventory model considers probabilistic demand for the situation where inventory cannot be carried from one period to the next. In a single-period inventory situation, one order is placed for the item; at the end of the period the item has either sold out or there is a surplus of unsold items, which will be sold for a salvage value. The single-period model applies to situations involving seasonal or perishable items that cannot be carried in inventory and sold in future periods.

The following three input values are required to use this model:

1. The cost of overestimating demand and ordering too much

2. The cost of underestimating demand and not ordering enough

3. The probability distribution for demand, which must be either a uniform or a normal probability distribution

The output information shows the optimal order quantity, the probability of a surplus, and the probability of a stockout.

CHAPTER 10

WAITING LINES

Waiting lines occur in many everyday situations. People wait in supermarket check-out lines, at bank teller windows, in doctor offices, at gasoline service stations, at airline ticket counters, and so on. In general, units (customers) arrive at a service facility seeking the service provided by the facility. If the service facility is busy, the units form a waiting line and wait until the service facility is available.

Quantitative models have been developed that enable decision makers to identify the operating characteristics of waiting line systems. Typical information provided by waiting line models includes the following:

1. The probability that the service facility is idle and there are no units in the system

2. The average number of units in the waiting line

3. The average number of units in the system (units waiting plus units being serviced)

4. The average time a unit spends in the waiting line

5. The average time a unit spends in the system (waiting time plus service time)

6. The probability that an arriving unit has to wait for service

7. The total system cost (the cost of idle time for the units in the system plus the cost of operating the service facility)

Given the above information, decision makers are better able to make waiting line design and policy decisions that balance the desired service levels with the cost of providing the service.

10.1 OVERVIEW

The Waiting Lines module of *The Management Scientist* provides the following five waiting line models.

1. *Single- or Multiple-Channel with Poisson Arrivals Exponential Service Times*— This is the fundamental waiting line model with Poisson arrivals and exponential service times. Operating characteristics are provided for systems having from 1 to 25 channels.

2. *Single-Channel with Poisson Arrivals and Arbitrary Service Times*—This model is restricted to a single-channel system. However, service times may follow *any* probability distribution. The only information needed about the service times is the mean service rate and the standard deviation of the service times.

3. *Single-Channel with Poisson Arrivals and Deterministic Service Times*— This model considers deterministic (constant) service times for a single-channel system. All units require the same amount of time; no variation in service time is permitted.

4. *Single- or Multiple-Channels with Poisson Arrivals, Arbitrary Service Times, and No Waiting Line*—This model considers situations where waiting is not permitted. An arriving unit either receives service immediately or is blocked from the system. Blocked units are not permitted to wait, are cleared from the system, and may try to re-enter at a later point in time. Operating characteristics are provided for systems having from 1 to 25 channels.

5. *Single- or Multiple-Channels with Poisson Arrivals, Exponential Service Times, and a Finite Calling Population*—In this waiting line model, a finite population of units is permitted to arrive for service. Populations with a maximum of 30 units are allowed. Operating characteristics are provided for systems having from 1 to 25 channels.

10.2 AN EXAMPLE PROBLEM

The Burger Dome fast-food restaurant operates a single-channel service facility for its customers. A single Burger Dome employee takes the customer's order, determines the total cost of the order, takes the money from the customer, and then fills the order. Once a customer's order is filled, the employee takes the order from the next customer waiting for service. The Poisson probability distribution describes the customer arrivals. The mean arrival rate is 0.75 customers per minute. The exponential probability distribution describes the service times. The mean service rate is one customer per minute. For economic considerations, Burger Dome evaluates customer waiting time at $10 per hour while the service channel can be operated for $7 per hour.

Management is interested in developing a better understanding of the operating characteristics of the food-service waiting line. Specifically, management would like to know the probability that no customers are in the system, the average number of customers waiting for service, the average time a customer waits for service, the probability that an arriving customer has to wait, and the hourly cost of the service operation.

10.3   CREATING AND SOLVING A PROBLEM

To solve the Burger Dome waiting line problem, we begin by selecting the Waiting Lines module and choosing New from the File menu; the Waiting Lines dialog box shown in Figure 10.1 will then appear. This dialog box can be used to select any one of the five waiting line models listed. Since the Burger Dome problem has a waiting line with Poisson arrivals and exponential service times, we select the Poisson Arrivals/Exponential Service model. The Poisson Arrivals/Exponential Service dialog box shown in Figure 10.2 appears on the screen. The data for the Burger Dome problem are entered with Number of Channels = 1, Mean Arrival Rate = .75, and Mean Service Rate = 1. Economic Analysis appears as a question since the waiting line model can be implemented with or without an economic analysis. Since the Burger Dome problem requested an economic analysis, the Economic Analysis box has been clicked on and the customer waiting time of $10 per hour and service channel cost of $7 per hour have been entered.

After the data input process is completed, Solve or Save can be implemented by selecting the appropriate button in the data input dialog box. Selecting Solve provides the

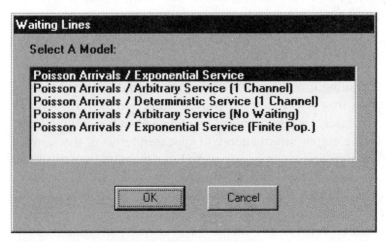

Figure 10.1   Waiting Lines Dialog Box

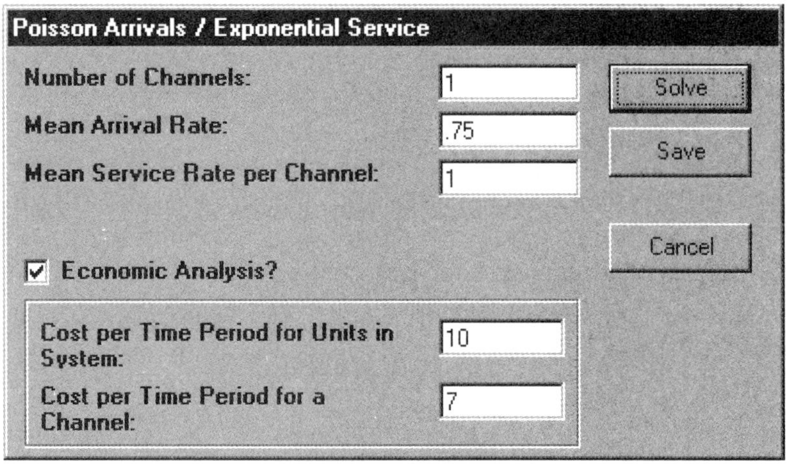

Figure 10.2   Poisson Arrivals/Exponential Service Dialog Box

output shown in Figure 10.3. While no direct recommendation is made, the output provides valuable information about the operating characteristics of the waiting line. An average of 2.25 customers are in the waiting line, the customers wait an average of three minutes for service, and .75 or 75% of the arriving customers have to wait for service. The total cost is $37.00 per hour. In addition, the probabilities of the number of customers in the system show that some long waiting lines are possible. The information in Figure 10.3 indicates that something should be done to improve the operation of the Burger Dome service facility.

Using the Edit menu, we can easily display the data input dialog box again and change the number of channels from 1 to 2. Selecting Solve shows the improved operating characteristics for the expanded Burger Dome service operation. The total cost of the two-channel system is $22.73 per hour. Repeating the edit process shows that the addition of a third channel with the total cost increasing to $28.65 per hour is not necessary.

10.4   OTHER CONSIDERATIONS

Each of the five models in the Waiting Lines module requires the input data to be based on the *same period of time*. The user may select the most convenient period of time such as a minute, hour, day, and so on. However, once selected, all input data must be stated in terms of the selected period of time. The output information will appear in terms of the selected time period. For example, if the user selects an hourly period of time, a mean arrival rate of 45 customers per hour and a mean service rate of 60 customers per hour will result in hourly output waiting times. On the other hand, if the user wanted to use a minute as the time period, the mean arrival rate would be converted to 45/60 = 0.75 customers per minute and the mean service rate would be converted to 60/60 = 1 customer per minute; in this case the output waiting times will be in minutes.

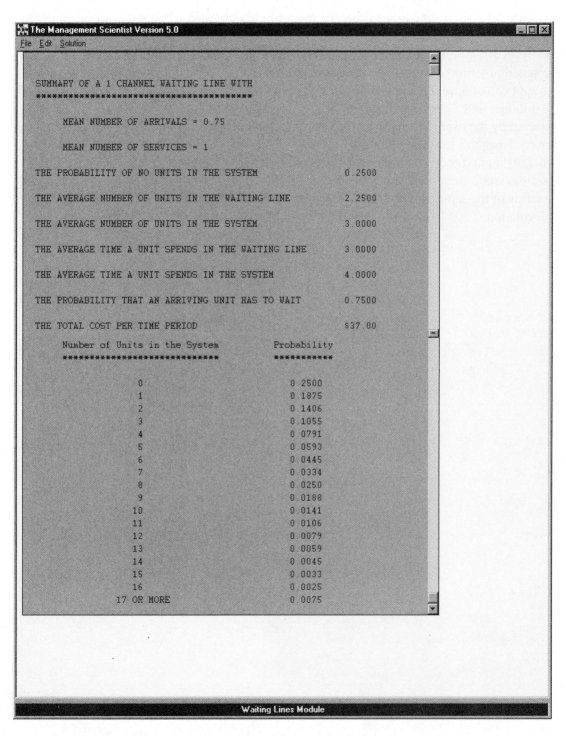

Figure 10.3   Output for the Burger Dome Waiting Line Problem

Model 2 allows the user to specify any arbitrary service time and requires care to ensure that proper units are maintained during the data input process. The data input requires the mean arrival rate, the mean service rate, and the standard deviation of service times to be stated in terms of the same period of time. For example, assume that data for a particular application have a mean arrival rate of two units per hour, service times with a mean of 20 minutes, and a standard deviation of 12 minutes. Assume that an hour is the time period selected by the user. The mean arrival rate is the stated two units per hour. However, on an hourly basis the mean service rate is $60/20 = 3$ units per hour. The standard deviation, which is input directly as time, must be converted to the same hourly basis. Thus the standard deviation of service times would be $12/60 = 0.20$ hour. If all the input is not stated in terms of the same unit of time, the module will provide incorrect and misleading output information.

CHAPTER 11

DECISION ANALYSIS

Decision analysis can be used to help a decision maker select the best decision alternative for problems involving several decision alternatives and an uncertain or risk-filled pattern of future events. A complicating factor in selecting the best alternative is that the future events, called *states of nature*, are uncontrollable; thus, the decision maker must select a decision alternative before knowing which state of nature will occur.

The following three steps can be used to structure a decision analysis problem:

1. Identify the decision alternatives

2. Identify the states of nature

3. Identify the payoff associated with each decision alternative and each state of nature combination

The above information can be summarized in a payoff table; the decision alternatives correspond to the rows of the table, the states of nature correspond to the columns of the table, and the payoffs are the values in each row and column.

The decision analysis approach to selecting the best decision alternative depends on whether or not probabilities are specified for the states of nature. If probabilities for the states of nature are *not* specified, the decision maker first selects one of several decision criteria; then, a decision alternative is recommended based on the criteria preference of the decision maker.

If probabilities for the states of nature are specified, decision analysis can be used to provide the following information:

1. The expected value or long-run average payoff for each decision alternative

2. A recommended decision alternative based on the best expected value

3. Expected value of perfect information—the expected value if the decision maker has the perfect information (i.e., the decision maker knows in advance which state of nature will occur)

In addition, decision analysis with probabilities provides the option of using sample information to revise the probabilities of the states of nature. In many cases a decision strategy based on the sample information can provide a better expected value.

11.1   OVERVIEW

The Decision Analysis module of *The Management Scientist* is designed to provide a recommended decision alternative for problems having the following characteristics:

1. Up to 10 decision alternatives

2. Up to 10 states of nature

3. Known or unknown state of nature probabilities

A variety of measures such as profit, cost, time, utility, and so on may be used for the payoff.

For decision making without probabilities, the decision maker has the choice of three decision criteria: optimistic, conservative, and minimax regret. The module will provide a recommended decision based on the criterion selected.

For decision making with probabilities, the module will provide a recommended decision based on the expected value criterion. Information is also provided for the expected value of perfect information.

When probabilities are used, an option is also provided for developing a decision strategy based on sample information. In this situation, sample information will guide the decision maker in selecting the best decision alternative. The module will identify the optimal decision strategy, its expected value, the expected value of the sample information, and the efficiency of the sample information.

11.2   AN EXAMPLE PROBLEM

Political Systems, Inc., (PSI) is a computer service firm specializing in information services such as surveys and data analysis for individuals running for political office. PSI is in the final stages of selecting a computer system for its Midwest office. The three decision alternatives PSI is considering are as follows:

d_1 = a large computer system

d_2 = a medium-sized computer system

d_3 = a small computer system

The uncertainty of the customer acceptance of the PSI service makes it difficult to know for sure which computer system the company should select. The following two states of nature for acceptance have been identified:

s_1 = high customer acceptance of the PSI services

s_2 = low customer acceptance of the PSI services

For now, assume that probability information is not available for the states of nature.

The payoff table showing the projected profit for each decision alternative and each state of nature combination is shown in Table 11.1. Given this information, which computer system should PSI select?

11.3   CREATING AND SOLVING A PROBLEM

To solve the PSI decision analysis problem, we begin by selecting the Decision Analysis module and choosing New from the File menu; the Problem Features dialog box will then appear. Figure 11.1 shows this dialog box after entering 3 for the Number of Decision Alternatives and 2 for the Number of States of Nature. For now, we will leave the State of Nature Probabilities turned off and analyze the PSI problem without using probability information. In Section 11.4 we will discuss the PSI problem when probability information is used.

After selecting OK in the Problem Features dialog box of Figure 11.1, we obtain the Payoff Table data input screen shown in Figure 11.2. Payoff data from Table 11.1 are entered into the corresponding cells of the Payoff Table as shown in Figure 11.2. When the

| | States of Nature | |
Decision Alternatives	High Acceptance	Low Acceptance
Large Computer System	200,000	–20,000
Medium-Sized Computer System	150,000	20,000
Small Computer System	100,000	60,000

Table 11.1   Payoff Table for the PSI Problem

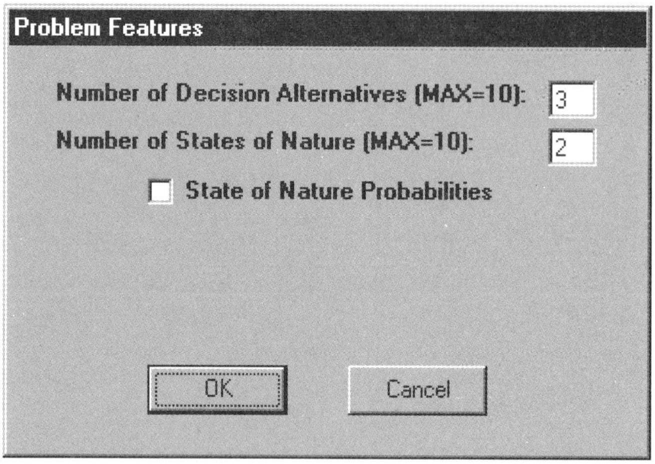

Figure 11.1   Problems Features Dialog Box

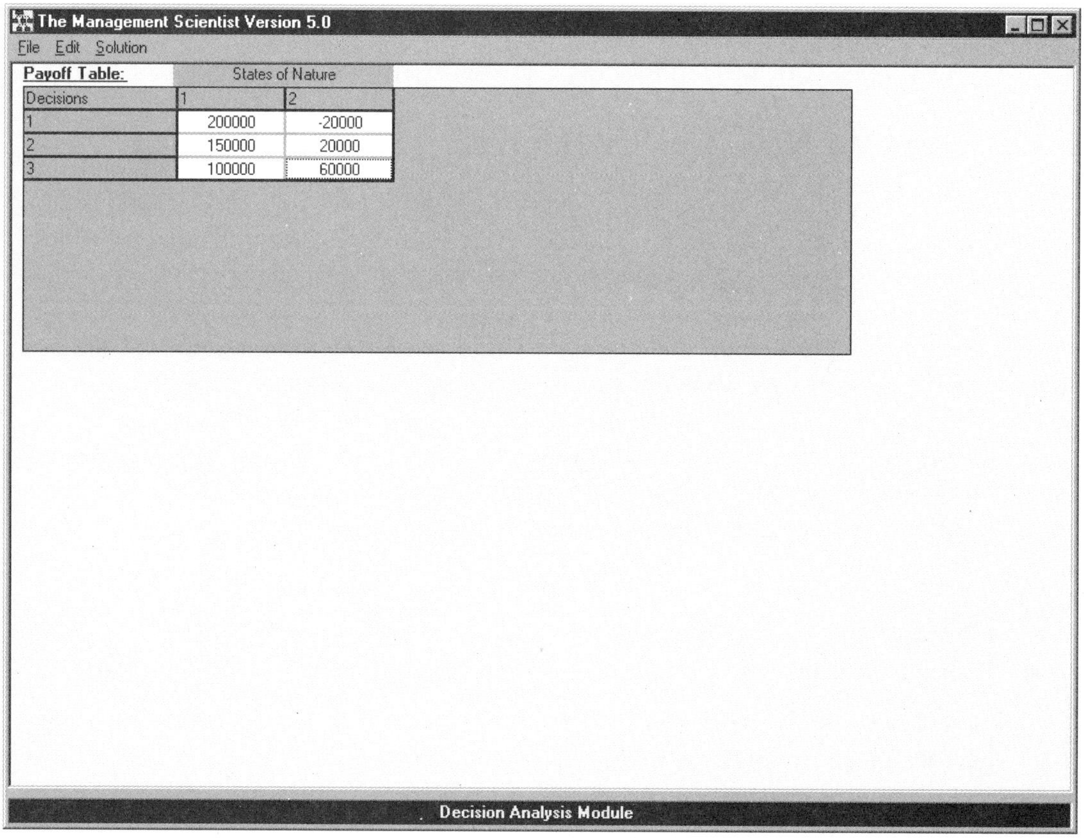

Figure 11.2   Data Input Screen for the PSI Problem

payoff data input process is completed, choosing Solve from the Solution menu provides the Select Optimization/Decision Criteria dialog box shown in Figure 11.3. For the PSI problem, we selected maximize the payoff as the optimization procedure and optimistic as the decision criterion. Selecting OK provides the output shown in Figure 11.4. The optimistic criterion recommends decision alternative 1, the large computer system.

11.4 USING PROBABILITY INFORMATION

Let us assume that state of nature probabilities are available for the PSI problem with the probability of high customer acceptance (state of nature 1) 0.3 and the probability of low customer acceptance (state of nature 2) 0.7. Decision analysis uses the probability information and the expected value criterion to make a decision recommendation.

With probability information available, *The Management Scientist* will consider this a new problem. Use the File menu and select New to obtain the Problem Features dialog box as shown in Figure 11.1. This time click the State of Nature Probabilities box. Selecting OK provides the Payoff Table data input screen shown in Figure 11.2 along with two additional cells used to enter the two state of nature probabilities. When the data input process is completed, choosing Solve from the Solution menu provides the Select Optimization Criteria dialog box, which enables the selection of a maximize or minimize criterion. Selecting maximize and then selecting OK provides the output shown in Figure 11.5 on page 75. In this case, decision alternative 3, the small computer system, is recommended. The expected value is $72,000. It is also shown that the expected value of perfect information is 30,000.

Sample Information and a Decision Strategy

If you are using state of nature probabilities, you will be given the option of selecting whether or not you would like to use sample information to develop a decision strategy.

Figure 11.3   Select Optimization/Decision Criteria Dialog Box

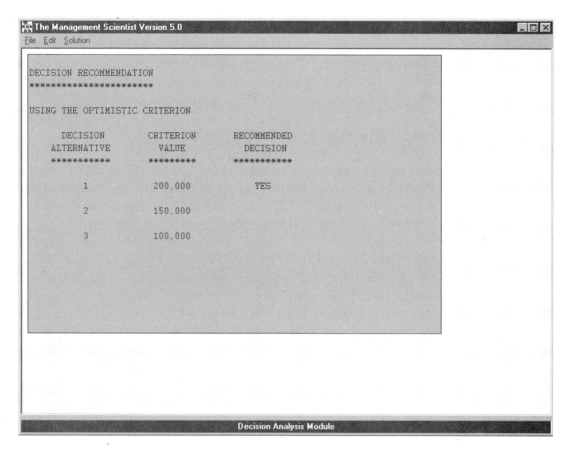

Figure 11.4   Output Information for the PSI Problem Using the Optimistic Criterion

Sample information usually takes the form of research or experimentation, which helps to better access the probabilities of the states of nature. Thus prior to selecting a decision alternative, sample information will be collected. This sample information will enable the revision of the state of nature probabilities. Ultimately, an optimal decision strategy will be computed; the strategy will show how the recommended decision alternative should be changed depending on the sample information.

Let us return to the PSI problem and assume that a marketing research study will be undertaken in order to obtain sample information about possible customer acceptance of the PSI service. The study is referred to as an *indicator*, and the results of the study are referred to as *indicator outcomes*. The two indicator outcomes for the PSI problem are as follows:

I_1 = favorable market research report (individuals contacted generally express considerable interest in PSI's services)

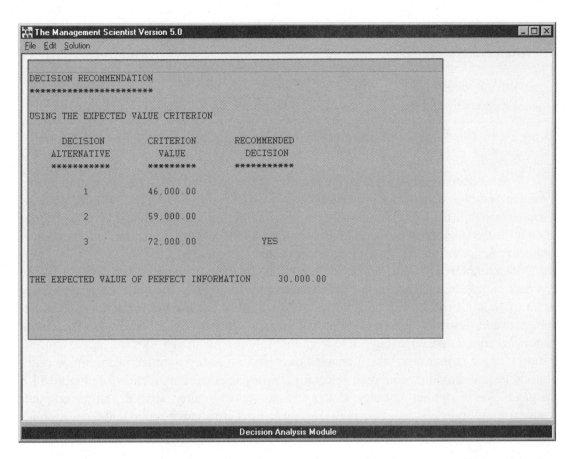

Figure 11.5   Output Information for the PSI Problem Using the Expected Value Criterion

I_2 = unfavorable market research report (individuals contacted generally express little interest in PSI's services)

In general, the use of sample information requires the identification of two or more indicator outcomes. In addition to specifying the indicator outcomes, we must also have information about the conditional probability of each indicator outcome for each state of nature. The conditional probability information for the PSI problem is shown in Table 11.2. For example, given state of nature 1 were to occur, there is a 0.8 probability the indicator outcome will be favorable and a 0.2 probability the indicator outcome will be unfavorable.

Let us now consider how the decision analysis module can be used to develop an optimal decision strategy based on the results of the market research indicator outcomes. In addition, we will determine the expected value of the sample information provided by the market research study.

States of Nature	Indicator Outcome	
	Favorable (I_1)	Unfavorable (I_2)
High acceptance (s_1)	0.8	0.2
Low acceptance (s_2)	0.1	0.9

Table 11.2 Conditional Probabilities of Indicator Outcomes for Each State of Nature

When a decision analysis problem requires the computation of a decision strategy, the Problem Features dialog box appears as shown in Figure 11.6. Note that both State of Nature Probabilities and Compute Decision Strategy have been clicked on. The values shown for the number of decision alternatives, number of states of nature, and number of indicator outcomes are for the PSI decision strategy problem.

Selecting OK provides the Payoff Table data input screen shown in Figure 11.7. The top part of the screen provides the payoff table input as before. The sections labeled Enter State of Nature Probabilities and Indicator Probabilities are used to input the state of nature probabilities and the indicator probabilities from Table 11.2. When the data input process is completed, choosing Solve from the Solution menu provides the Select Optimization Criteria dialog box, which enables the selection of a maximize or minimize criterion. Selecting maximize and then selecting OK provides the output shown in Figure 11.8 on page 78. The optimal decision strategy shows decision alternative d_1 (large computer system) if the indicator outcome is I_1 (favorable market research report), and decision alternative d_3 (small computer system) if the indicator outcome is I_2 (unfavorable market research report).

Problem Features

Number of Decision Alternatives (MAX=10): 3

Number of States of Nature (MAX=10): 2

☑ State of Nature Probabilities

☑ Compute Decision Strategy
  (If Yes, Indicator Probabilities are Requested.)

Number of Indicator Outcomes (MAX=10): 2

OK   Cancel

Figure 11.6 Problem Features Dialog Box for the PSI Decision Strategy Problem

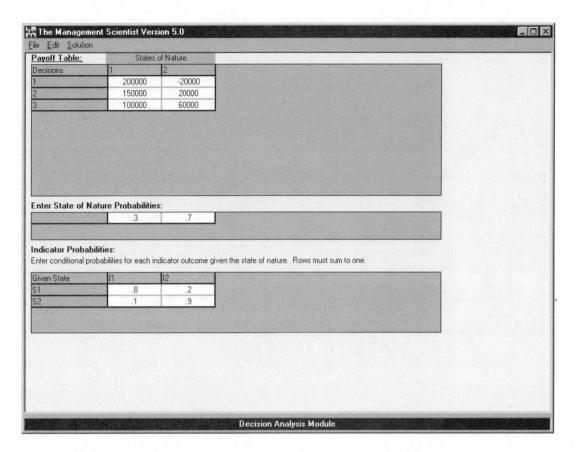

Figure 11.7 Data Input Screen for the PSI Decision Strategy Problem

Additional output information shows that if indicator outcome I_1 occurs the expected profit will be \$150,322.58. The probability of this indicator outcome is 0.31. Also note that if indicator outcome I_2 occurs, the expected profit will be \$63,478.26. The probability of this indicator outcome is 0.69. The expected value of the decision strategy using the indicator outcome information is \$90,400. Thus the expected value of the market research sample information is \$18,400. The value of sample information is 61.3% of the value that could be obtained with perfect information.

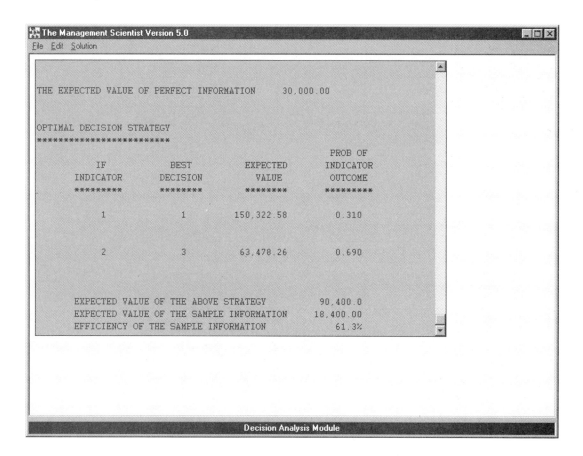

Figure 11.8   Optimal Decision Strategy for PSI

CHAPTER 12

FORECASTING

A critical aspect of managing any organization is planning for the future. Indeed, the long-run success of an organization is closely related to how well management is able to foresee the future and develop appropriate strategies. Forecasting techniques are available to help managers predict many future aspects of a business operation.

Historical data on quantities such as sales, demand, stock prices, university enrollments, and so on are collected over time and form what are called *time series*. Specifically, a time series is a set of observations measured at successive points in time or over successive periods of time. The manager who wishes to forecast a particular time series will find that the historical values of the time series provide clues about future values.

Quantitative forecasting methods are based on an analysis of historical data. When the historical data used is restricted to past values in the time series being forecasted, the forecasting procedure is called a time series method.

12.1   OVERVIEW

The Forecasting module of *The Management Scientist* can be used to analyze time series data consisting of up to 100 time periods or observations. Future values of the time series may be forecast by any of the following methods:

1. *Moving Averages*—This method uses the average of the most recent data values to forecast the next value for the time series. The number of data values in the moving average forecast must be specified by the user.

2. *Exponential Smoothing*—This method uses a combination of the forecast for the most recent period and the actual time series value for the most recent period to forecast the next value for the time series. The weight used for the most recent time series value is referred to as the *smoothing constant* and must be specified by the user.

3. *Trend Projection*—This method uses the criterion of least squares to develop a linear trend equation, which expresses the time series values as a linear function of the time period. Forecasts are made by evaluating the linear trend equation for future time periods.

4. *Trend and Seasonal Components*—This method applies to a time series that has both trend and seasonality. First the seasonal influence is removed from the time series by a process referred to as *deseasonalizing* the data. Then the criterion of least squares is used to develop a linear trend equation, which expresses the deseasonalized time series as a linear function of the time period. The linear trend equation is used to forecast future values for the deseasonalized time series. Finally, an adjustment for the seasonality of the time period provides the forecast for the time series.

A given time series may be analyzed by one or more of the above forecasting methods. A comparison of forecasting accuracy for the methods will indicate which method appears to have the best potential for forecasting future values of the time series.

12.2   AN EXAMPLE PROBLEM: FORECASTING USING MOVING AVERAGES

Consider the 12 weeks of data presented in Table 12.1. These data provide a time series of the number of gallons of gasoline sold by a gasoline distributor in Bennington, Vermont, over the past 12 weeks. Use the method of moving averages to forecast the number of gallons of gasoline that will be sold in week 13.

12.3   CREATING AND SOLVING A PROBLEM

To forecast the number of gallons of gasoline that will be sold in week 13 for the time series shown in Table 12.1, we begin by selecting the Forecasting module and choosing New from the File menu. When the Time Periods dialog box appears, enter 12 for the Number of Time Periods and choose OK; these steps result in the data input screen. Figure 12.1 shows the data input screen after entering the gasoline sales time series data. After selecting Solve from the Solution menu, we obtain the Forecasting Methods dialog box shown in Figure 12.2. Any one of the four methods listed may be used to forecast values for the time series.

If Moving Averages is selected, you must enter the Number of Periods to be included in the moving average. While any number of periods from 1 to the number of periods in

Week	Sales (1000s of Gallons)
1	17
2	21
3	19
4	23
5	18
6	16
7	20
8	18
9	22
10	20
11	15
12	22

Table 12.1   A Time Series of Gasoline Sales

the time series (12 in this example) may be used in the moving average, values of 3 to 5 tend to be most common. In order to continue this example, we used 3 as the number of periods to be included in the moving average.

After you specify the number of periods for the moving average and click Solve, the Forecasting module provides a summary of the three-week moving average calculations for the gasoline time series; Figure 12.3 on page 83 shows the output provided. The time series values, the moving averages forecasts, and the forecast errors are shown for the entire time series. Since an important consideration in using any forecasting method is the accuracy of the forecasts, the *mean square error* (MSE), an often used measure of the accuracy of a forecasting method, is also provided. The forecasting method providing the lowest mean square error has provided the best forecasts for the historical time series values. Also shown is the forecast for the next period in the time series. Thus, we see that the three-period moving averages forecast for week 13 is 19,000 gallons.

12.4   OTHER FORECASTING METHODS

The Forecasting module contains four methods that may be used to develop forecasts for a time series. These methods are made available by the Forecasting Methods dialog box shown in Figure 12.2. An example of the moving averages method was presented in the preceding section. In this section we provide an overview of each of the other three methods. We will describe the method and then discuss the data input and output information features that differ from the moving averages example in Section 12.3.

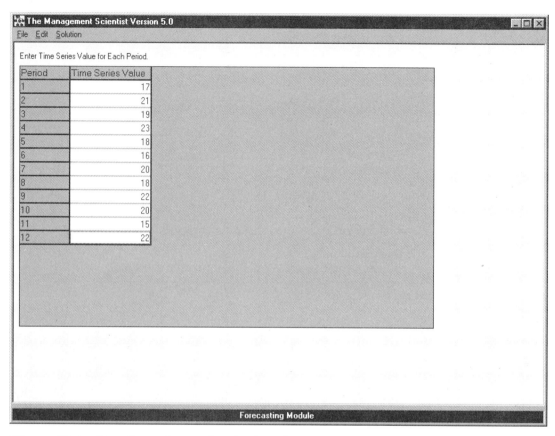

Figure 12.1 Data Input Screen for the Gasoline Sales Time Series

Figure 12.2 Forecasting Methods Dialog Box

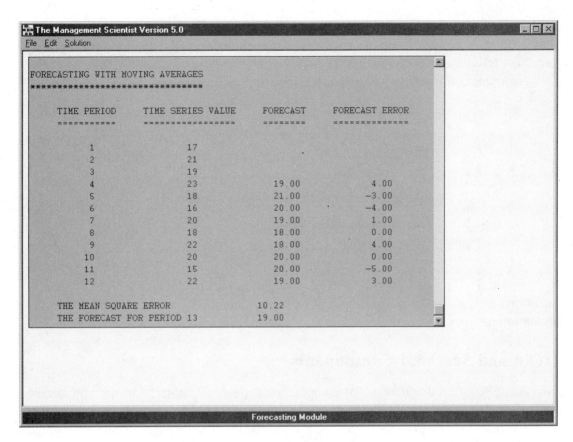

Figure 12.3   The Forecasting Error and Forecast for the 3-Week Moving Averages

Exponential Smoothing

Exponential smoothing appears as choice 2 in the Forecasting Methods dialog box in Figure 12.2. This method uses a combination of the forecast for the most recent period and the actual time series value for the most recent period to forecast the next value for the time series. The weight used for the most recent time series value is referred to as the *smoothing constant*. If you select the exponential smoothing method, you will be asked to enter the value of the smoothing constant. This value must be between 0 and 1.

Output information includes the time series values, the exponential smoothing forecast, and the forecast errors for the historical time series. In addition, the mean square error and the forecast for the next time period are also provided.

Trend Projection

Trend projection appears as choice 3 in the Forecasting Methods dialog box shown in Figure 12.2. This method uses the criterion of least squares to develop a linear trend equation, which expresses the time series values as a linear function of the time period. The trend projection analysis begins as soon as this option is selected. No additional input information is required.

The output information will provide a linear trend equation in the form

$$T = b_0 + b_1 t$$

where

t	$=$	the time period
T	$=$	the trend value of the time series in period t
b_0	$=$	the intercept of the trend line
b_1	$=$	the slope of the trend line

The numerical values of b_0 and b_1 will be provided as part of the output. Additional output information is similar to the output provided by the moving averages and exponential smoothing routines.

Trend and Seasonal Components

Forecasting with trend and seasonal components appears as choice 4 in the Forecasting Methods dialog box shown in Figure 12.2. This method should be used for time series that are believed to have both *linear* trend and seasonality. If you select this forecasting method you will be asked to enter the number of seasonal indexes to be computed. In order to do this you must have an idea of how many seasons are present in the time series. The forecasting method will develop a seasonal index for each season present. If you have a time series with monthly data for several years, you will probably request 12 seasonal indexes to consider the possibility that each month has a different seasonal effect. If you have a time series with quarterly data for several years, you will probably request 4 seasonal indexes to consider the possibility that each quarter has a different seasonal effect.

After you enter the number of seasonal indexes, the output will appear on the screen in three separate sections. The first section will provide the seasonal indexes. Figure 12.4 shows an example of this output for a time series with quarterly data. The fourth quarter with an index of 1.141 shows that the time series is 114.1% higher in this quarter when the seasonal influence is considered. The second quarter with an index of 0.836 shows that the time series will tend to be lower than normal in this quarter. The other output sections follow the format of Figure 12.3; that is, the past time series values, the forecasts, the forecast errors, the mean square error, and the forecasts for each of the next three time periods are provided, as well as an option of forecasting additional periods in the future. Simply request this option, enter the time period you wish to forecast, and the Forecasting module will provide the forecast.

FORECASTING WITH TREND AND SEASONAL COMPONENTS

SEASON	SEASONAL INDEX
1	0.931
2	0.836
3	1.092
4	1.141

Figure 12.4   An Example with Four Seasonal Indexes

CHAPTER 13

MARKOV PROCESSES

The analysis of brand loyalty and brand switching behavior is one of the major applications of Markov processes. In this application, the purchase decision that is made each time period by a customer involves selecting one of several competing brands. The brands are referred to as the *states* of the process. Given that the customer has purchased a specific brand during the current time period, *transition probabilities* describe the probabilities that the customer will purchase the same brand as well as each of the competing brands during the following time period.

The transition probability for a given state to itself is a measure of brand loyalty in that it indicates the probability that the customer will purchase the same brand in two successive periods. The transition probabilities for a given state to each of the other states measure the brand switching behaviors of the customer. Based on known or assumed transition probabilities, a Markov process model can be used to answer questions such as the following:

1. In the long run, what market share will each brand have?

2. If a new and/or improved brand enters the market, what impact can be expected on the market share of each brand?

3. For a given group of customers, how many will purchase each brand each time period?

Markov process models have also been developed for machine breakdown behavior, estimating allowances for bad debt, and university enrollment projections. In each instance it is assumed that (1) there are a finite number of states, (2) the transition probabilities remain constant over time, and (3) the probability of being in a particular state at any one time period depends only on the state of the process during the preceding time period.

13.1 OVERVIEW

The Markov processes module of *The Management Scientist* will analyze problems with up to 10 states. Input to the program is the matrix of transition probabilities for the states. The solution provides the steady-state probabilities for the states.

In some applications it may not be possible to make a transition out of one or more states once the state has been reached. Such states are referred to as *absorbing states*. The Markov processes module will solve problems for which the total number of absorbing and nonabsorbing states is 10 or less. In applications with absorbing states, the solution provides the probability that units currently in each of the nonabsorbing states will eventually end up in each of the absorbing states.

13.2 AN EXAMPLE PROBLEM

Two grocery stores in a small town compete for customers. Each customer makes one shopping trip per week to one of the two stores. A survey of store loyalty among the customers shows that for customers who shop at Murphy's Foodliner one week, 90% will shop at Murphy's the next week and 10% will switch to Ashley's Supermarket. For customers who shop at Ashley's Supermarket one week, 20% will switch to Murphy's the next week and 80% will shop again at Ashley's. These transition probabilities are summarized as follows:

Current Weekly Shopping Period	Next Weekly Shopping Period	
	Murphy's Foodliner	Ashley's Supermarket
Murphy's Foodliner	0.9	0.1
Ashley's Supermarket	0.2	0.8

What are the steady-state probabilities for the two grocery stores? If there are 1,000 customers that make weekly shopping trips to one of the two stores, how many customers can be expected to shop at each of the stores?

13.3 CREATING AND SOLVING A PROBLEM

To determine the steady-state probabilities for the two grocery stores in our example problem, we begin by selecting the Markov processes module and choosing New from the File menu. When the Markov Processes dialog box appears, enter 2 for the Number of States and choose OK; the Transition Matrix data input screen will then appear. Figure 13.1 shows the Transition Matrix after entering the transition probabilities for the grocery store

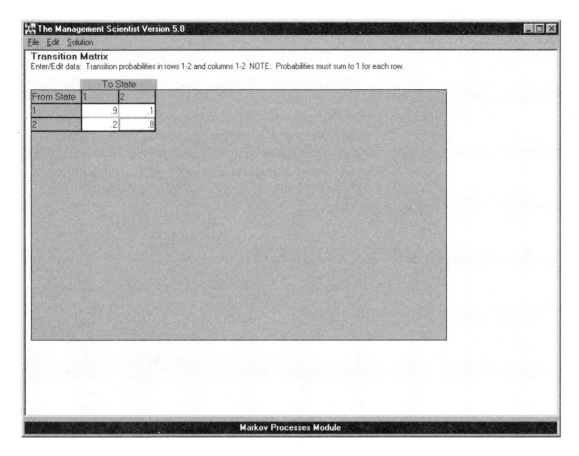

Figure 13.1   Transition Matrix Data Input Screen

example problem. After selecting Solve from the Solution menu, we obtain the output shown in Figure 13.2.

As you can see, Murphy's Foodliner (state 1) has the higher steady-state probability. Thus, we conclude that in the long run, Murphy's Foodliner will have a 66.7% share of the market and Ashley's Supermarket will have the remaining 33.3% share of the market. With 1,000 weekly customers, 667 should shop at Murphy's and 333 should shop at Ashley's.

13.4   AN EXAMPLE PROBLEM WITH ABSORBING STATES

Heidman's Department Stores has two aging categories for its accounts receivable: (1) accounts that are classified as 0 to 30 days old and (2) accounts that are classified as 31 to 90 days old. If any portion of an account balance exceeds 90 days, that portion is written off as a bad debt. The total account balance for each customer is placed in the age category

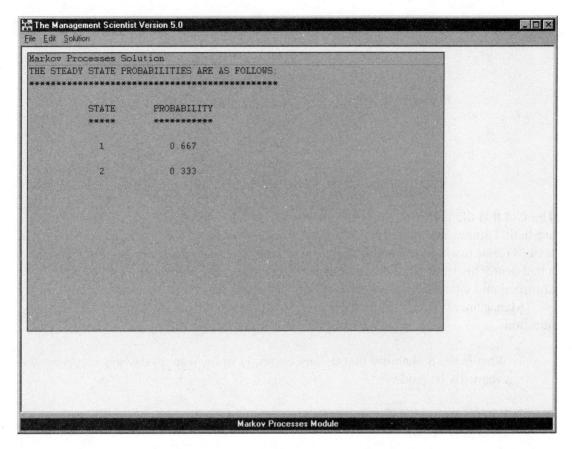

Figure 13.2   Output for the Grocery Store Market Share Problem

corresponding to the oldest unpaid amount; hence, this method of aging accounts receivable is called the *total balance method.*

Let us assume that Heidman's shows a total of $3,000 in its accounts receivable and the firm's management would like an estimate of how much of the $3,000 will eventually be collected and how much will result in bad debts.

To see how we can view the accounts receivable operation as a Markov process, consider what happens to *one* dollar currently in accounts receivable. As the firm continues to operate into the future, we can consider each week as a trial of a Markov process with a dollar existing in one of the following states of the system:

State	Description
1	Paid category
2	Bad debt category
3	0 to 30 days age category
4	31 to 90 days age category

Based on historical transitions of accounts receivable dollars, the following transition probabilities were developed for Heidman's Department Stores:

From State	To State			
	1	2	3	4
1	1.0	0.0	0.0	0.0
2	0.0	1.0	0.0	0.0
3	0.4	0.0	0.3	0.3
4	0.4	0.2	0.3	0.1

The fact that the transition probabilities from state 1 to state 1 and from state 2 to state 2 are both 1 shows that these two states are absorbing states. That is, once a dollar is paid (state 1) it is always paid. Similarly, once a dollar is declared a bad debt (state 2), it remains a bad debt. This leads us to conclude that all accounts receivable dollars will eventually be absorbed into either the paid or the bad debt state, and hence the name *absorbing state*.

Management of Heidman's Department Stores would like to answer the following questions:

1. What is the probability that dollars currently in the 0 to 30 day age category will eventually be paid?

2. What is the probability that dollars currently in the 31 to 90 day age category will eventually be paid?

3. If $1,000 is currently in the 0 to 30 day category and $2,000 is currently in the 31 to 90 day category, how much will be paid and how much will end up as bad debt?

The problem creation step for this problem is the same as that described previously. No special input procedures are required to handle the absorbing states. The output is shown in Figure 13.3. There is a .889 probability that the 0 to 30 day age category dollars will be paid and a .741 probability that the 31 to 90 day age category dollars will be paid. Thus, of the current $3,000 of account receivables, the amount paid is projected to be .889($1,000) + .741($2,000) = $2,371. An allowance for bad debt should be set up for $3,000 − $2,371 = $639.

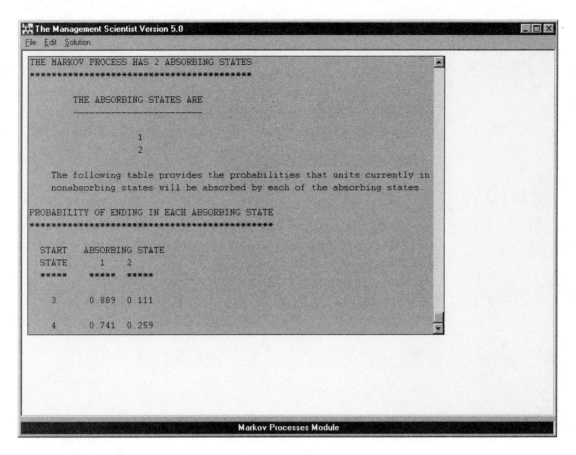

Figure 13.3   Output for the Accounts Receivable Problem